P9-DNS-714

DISCARGE
LIBRARY

353.0072 K849id
Koven, Steven G.
Ideological budgeting

Ideological Budgeting

The Influence of
Political Philosophy
on Public Policy

Steven G. Koven

PRAEGER

New York
Westport, Connecticut
London

To Andrea and Eli

Library of Congress Cataloging-in-Publication Data

Koven, Steven G.
  Ideological budgeting.

  Bibliography: p.
  Includes index.
  1. Budget—Political aspects—United States.
2. Right and left (Political science) I. Title.
HJ2051.K68   1988   353.0072'221   87-38502
ISBN 0-275-92946-9 (alk. paper)

Copyright © 1988 by Steven G. Koven

All rights reserved. No portion of this book may
be reproduced, by any process or technique, without
the express written consent of the publisher.

Library of Congress Catalog Card Number: 87-38502
ISBN: 0-275-92946-9

First published in 1988

Praeger Publishers, One Madison Avenue, New York, NY 10010
A division of Greenwood Press, Inc.

Printed in the United States of America

The paper used in this book complies with the
Permanent Paper Standard issued by the National
Information Standards Organization (Z39.48-1984).

10 9 8 7 6 5 4 3 2 1

Contents

Tables and Figures

TABLES

Part I

INFLUENCES OF IDEOLOGY

1

Introduction

In the narrow sense, budgeting conjures up images of men in thick glasses counting endless series of receipts and posting entries to endless numbers of journals. With some justification budgeting is viewed as a boring, lifeless pursuit. This cannot be further from the truth. Viewed in a broader context, budgeting defines our priorities; it reflects our inner beliefs and guides our behavior. Budgets establish the winners and losers in policy debates that shape the future of our collective society. Budget debate defines the playing field on which power and status are ultimately determined. Budgeting in the broad sense also decides who will be able to transform their visions into reality and who will see their dreams evaporate or slowly erode as their priorities become perceived as irrelevant, impractical, or misguided; while the priorities of others capture the public policy agenda.

The fundamental questions posed in the budgetary process remain unchanged by the passage of time. Budgeters ask how to maximize the value of scarce resources, how to make comparisons between competing demands, how to raise revenue, and how to determine aggregate spending levels. Definitive answers to these questions are not always available. A reason for this deficiency is the fact that budgeting deals with values and power relationships as well as administrative prescriptions. The political considerations of budgeting may in fact be more important than anything else. The importance of politics and political philosophy to public policy outputs is described in this book.

In the public sector, neutral evaluations of the success of an organization are not guaranteed. Different analysts may even hold different views concerning how success is determined. For example, professional policy analysts as well as average citizens are likely to have difficulty evaluating the effectiveness of their state's Department of Transportation or their nation's Department of Defense. Furthermore, evidence of poor public sector performance, such as the failed launch by the National Aeronautics and Space Administration (NASA) in 1986, does not always translate into the same outcomes as one would expect for the private sector. Poor performance will not necessarily result in lower spending levels in a public agency. On the contrary, as the NASA example demonstrates, poor performance may result in sharply increased budget allocations to make up for past failures.

NASA's allocations were to increase as a result of the decision to purchase a new spacecraft to replace the vehicle that exploded. In the private sector a company with a poor track record of orbiting spacecraft would lose customers, be forced to cut spending, and in the extreme case be forced into bankruptcy. Obviously, great differences exist in terms of spending determinations between the private and public sectors. Another example of the phenomenon of public sector failure leading to increased allocation levels is the failed attempt to free U.S. hostages from Iran in 1980. In the years immediately following the death of eight U.S. crewmen killed in an accidental collision between a helicopter and a transport plane, military spending increased by a considerable margin.

One can see from this paradox that application of private sector standards to public sector budgets may be impossible. Growth in public sector agencies appears to be a function of public perception of need and legislative willingness to meet that need. Growth in the private sector appears to be more a function of the willingness of buyers in the marketplace to purchase specific goods or services. Perception of need in the private sector must be backed by purchasing power. Organizational growth and allocations in the private sector are determined by factors such as yearly profit. Organizational growth and allocations in the public sector are determined by other factors. These are likely to be more political than rational.

The commonly recognized goal of profit is not applicable to the public sector. How, then, do public sector policy analysts and budgeters assess the policy effectiveness of resource allocation? A number of different perspectives exist from which to study resource allocation in the public sector. One of these perspectives is incrementalism.

The incremental perspective suggests that in order to find out how much to spend on a particular good or service, the best method is to identify how much was spent on that item in the preceding year. Barring any catastrophe, the safest and least controversial manner of deciding who gets what is to give everyone what they received in the prior year, plus a little more to account for inflation and marginal growth. In this incremental scenario there are no real winners or losers and budgeters do not have to go through the difficult and emotionally draining task of informing certain agencies that they have been targeted for bigger decreases or smaller increases than others. Furthermore, in the incremental budgeting scenario analysts do not have to go through the difficult process of evaluating agencies and objectively quantifying needs. Incrementalism, in short, is a seductively appealing concept to budgeters because it makes their job relatively easy. All that is needed is a pocket calculator and a copy of the previous year's budget. Incrementalism, however, is limited in that it does not reflect priority changes that occur over time.

If an individual were to look at his or her life from one minute to the next, chances are great that everything would look about the same. Yet, if one were to look at one's life over a broad span of years, chances are great that some change did occur. One probably would have more or less money today than 20 years ago, more or less responsibility, more or fewer expenses, and more or less debt. In the same regard, our society is not static but dynamic, with different options to choose from and new challenges to confront.

Budgets and budgeters must meet the fresh challenges and problems that arise in different eras. Unfortunately, the concept of incrementalism does not provide a mechanism for meeting those challenges because it merely states that current allocations usually approximate allocation levels in previous periods. Because of this bias to reinforce what already exists, incrementalism is useless as a policy tool to explain dynamic change. In periods of change, public opinion and political behavior seem to be more useful as tools for explaining shifts in resource allocations than does the static prescription of incrementalism.

U.S. budget priorities and levels of spending have changed considerably over the years. In the nation's formative years, the public sector was only a fraction of its present size. In fiscal year 1912–13 federal spending accounted for only 2 percent of the nation's gross national product.[1] In 1984–85 this proportion had risen to more than 23 percent. The rise in federal spending was aided by the introduction of a uniform and nationwide income tax in 1913. The income tax quickly became a mainstay of our federal revenue structure and the size of public budgets expanded considerably.

Federal acceptance of responsibility in areas such as unemployment compensation, aid to the elderly, health care for the poor, and public assistance illustrates how the size and shape of public sector budgets can change over time. The launch of the Russian satellite Sputnik in 1959 generated a significant change in the attitude of the federal government in regard to education and space exploration. Federal government spending in both areas expanded in the post–1959 period.

The Soviet invasion of Afghanistan and the hostage crisis in Iran probably created the environment for recent large increases in U.S. defense expenditures. This is but another example of change in established practices in contrast to reinforcement of the status quo which emanates from incremental strategies. As a result of these changes, one can conclude that a budget analyst falling asleep in 1930 and waking up in 1980 would have a hard time comprehending the changes that have occurred in our nation's spending patterns and priorities.

Incrementalism by itself is not able to explain change. It is not structured to explain societal response to exogenous shocks from the environment. Government reaction to sudden environmental change, however, is an empirical fact. Viewed in the broad historical context, response to change in environments seems to be a superior method of understanding budgetary behavior compared to incrementalism. Incrementalism remains an appealing concept, but its applicability is limited to periods of relative stability. Its fatal flaw seems to be its inability to explain the dynamics of allocation decisions, namely its inability to answer the questions of why and how changes occur in spending.

A second approach to the study of budgeting is found in the so-called political perspective. This perspective of budgeting focuses upon the bargaining and negotiating that occur between budget actors in the process of resource allocation. The political perspective is somewhat complex and can be broken down into a number of components. Elections, legislative behavior, bureaucratic interests, political ideology, individual interests, and lobbying all influence public sector budgeting. When these political factors are considered, budgeting is viewed from the perspective of being the result of bargaining and compromise between competing forces in society. This view rejects the perspective of so-called scientific analysis that characterizes the rational perspective and accepts the perspective of outputs resulting from the conflict over who is able to get his or her policy preferences implemented and who has the power to shape events.

Elections shape budgets because they determine which candidate and which preference will prevail to exert influence on policy. For example, if in a gubernatorial race one candidate ran on the promise to double the capacity of the state's prisons and the other candidate promised to maintain current prison capacity levels, we could surmise that the electorate could determine spending priorities through their choice of one candidate over the other. Power would be derived from the people if the candidate, once elected, actually carried out his or her campaign promises. This is often, however, a hazardous assumption; yet from the perspective of democratic theory, this scenario is viewed positively because power can ultimately be traced back to the citizenry.

A second perception of political budgeting involves the behavior of legislators. Legislators are well known for their logrolling or trading votes in order to secure pork-barrel legislation. This type of legislation results in passage of bills that will secure benefits for constituents back home. Budgeting under this perspective is more a test of a legislator's ability to bring tangible benefits to constituents than of his or her ability to pass sound and responsible budgets. Legislators who secure benefits, whether needed or not, are likely to be rewarded by constituents and returned to office. There is some logic to this madness at the individual legislative level; however, in the aggregate sense, rational choices may not occur when all legislators seek to maximize constituent benefits irrespective of the aggregate needs of society.

Another perception of political budgeting involves the role bureaucratic interests play in determining outputs. Career bureaucrats invariably prefer larger budgets for their agencies and support policy changes that will lead to these ends.[2] Bureaucrats become advocates for specific public sector action. As advocates of their chosen agency, they desire bigger budgets, larger staffs, and other responsibilities that will lead to larger salaries, larger offices, and more prestige. The goal of optimizing scarce resources is replaced by the bureaucratic priorities of power and prestige.

Political ideology also affects budgeting because ideology shapes values and these values in turn shape spending priorities. V. O. Key, Jr. recognized this link between values and budget priorities back in 1940. William Gorham also identified this phenomenon during testimony before the Joint Economic Committee in 1967. Gorham accurately noted that the "grand decisions" such as how much health, how much education, how much welfare, and which groups in society should benefit were really questions of value judgment.[3]

Individual interests may also have a subtle but pervasive effect on budgeting. For example, if you are the head of an agency and your best friend is in charge of a department within your agency, the personal relationship that you have developed with your friend can either subtly or overtly influence funding decisions. Other personal relationships that develop in an organization can also be a determining factor when the time comes to make allocation decisions. For example, if an agency head and co-worker are having an affair, funds of the department may be made available for more conferences so that the two can meet conveniently at the company's expense. With the vast number of funding decisions that must be made, individual interests cannot be ignored in regard to the role they play in shaping organizational allocations.

Finally, lobbying can influence budget allocations. Lobbyists attempt to shape budget priorities in favor of private clients. They may contribute to political campaigns or even offer bribes in order to gain personal advantage. These advocates of special interests are not likely to represent the public good. Their allegiance is to private supporters who demand tangible results as a payback for the substantial fees lobbyists charge. Lobbyists can distort rationality in the budgetary process if they are powerful enough to have clients' interests prevail over the interests of the general public. Rationality in terms of allocational analysis that will result in the greatest good for the greatest number is willingly sacrificed by lobbyists at the altar of personal gain.

Lobbyists, like legislators, serve particular groups. They are employed by private interest groups while legislators work for the benefit of their constituents. It is assumed that successful lobbyists provide tangible benefits to clients and that popular legislators "bring home the bacon" to constituents. It is conceivable that popular legislators also look after the nation's good as well as that of their constituents. It is less likely, however, that the interests of the public good would be of great concern to lobbyists; certainly they will be secondary to the interests of clients. In such a scenario the public good invariably suffers. It is logical to conclude that the most efficient and equitable use of the nation's resources does not occur when lobbyists proliferate in the nation's capital and legislators line up at the trough to feed off of public projects.

A third perspective from which to view budgeting is as a rational process of decision making. According to this perspective, budgeters employ empirical techniques to optimize the allocation of scarce resources. This perspective follows principles of economics and assumes that subjective values can be quantified. Once values are quantified, budgetary problems are solved, as one would solve a problem in mathematics or physics. Through rational, comprehensive analysis it is assumed that one can objectively determine proper levels of spending and maximize the social good for society. Over time, various rational techniques for budgeting have been developed. The success of these techniques, however, has been at best limited.

The most popular rational budgetary techniques, according

to leading authorities, are planning programming budgeting (PPB), management by objective (MBO), and zero-based budgeting (ZBB). Each of these techniques enjoyed periods of respectability, but eventually all were discredited.

PPB differed from traditional budgeting in that the ethos of budgeting shifted from justification to analysis. Under the PPB budget technique, decisions were influenced by explicit statements of objectives and by a formal weighing of the costs and benefits of alternatives.[4] PPB sought greater rationality in budgeting, attempted to improve planning prior to spending, and tried to make programs rather than agencies the central focus of budgeting. Conceivably the waste and duplication that arose from many agencies dealing with the same problem or the same program could be eliminated.

In the early 1960s there was a great deal of enthusiasm for PPB and its ability to improve government management. Hard appraisals of objectives and alternatives as well as multiyear budget plans were expected to make government operations more efficient. Those high hopes were not realized.

A number of explanations can be cited for the demise of this budget innovation. Perhaps the most damaging critique of PPB was the allegation that it was too vague and confusing. Aaron Wildavsky stated that tremendous confusion surrounded PPB, that it piled meaningless data into vague categories, and that it resembled a Rube Goldberg contraption.[5] PPB also had serious interagency implications. It strengthened the role of technicians such as economists, computer programmers, and mathematicians while decreasing the influence of "older" managers who previously held power. The threat to the older generation of decision makers was eventually repulsed and PPB's influence waned.

Management by objective (MBO) was also based on the use of objectivity and rationality in the budgetary process. The technical underpinnings of MBO, however, were simpler than those of PPB. Management by objective required agency administrators to identify their objectives in terms of simple targets, and they were then to be held accountable to those targets. Dissatisfaction inevitably also developed with this newer technique of budgeting. One problem that arose in MBO relates to the difficulty of setting concrete objectives in the public sector. It is recognized that clarity of goals is a practice vigorously pursued in the private sector, where the profit motive is preeminent and accountability is clearer. Clarity of goals in the public sector is more problematic and less common. This may be attributed to the fact that stating goals too specifically in the public sector may upset coalitions that hang together on the basis of ambiguous conceptualizations. Alliances may fall apart if goals are stated in clearly understood language. Managers of public agencies also have a vested interest in keeping statements of goals vague. If goals were ambiguous, managers could not be held accountable for not achieving them.

Another problem with MBO was the tendency to state goals in terms of outputs, such as the number of claims filed by an unemployment office or the number of miles of highway paved. This strategy has the limitation of not measuring quality of service delivery.[6] Assessments of public sector success were limited to these easily quantifiable measures. It did not matter whether or not recipients at an unemployment office were unhappy with the service delivered to them, or whether a paved highway would fall apart in six months, if only quantitative measures were considered and qualitative factors ignored. This was a major flaw of management by objective. It is conceivable that MBO might have been a more effective tool if more qualitative as well as quantitative measures were considered and public sector managers were more willing to specify objectives.

Zero-base budgeting (ZBB) is the newest of the three rational budgeting tools. ZBB was first implemented in the private sector at Texas Instruments. Public sector application began in Georgia under the administration of Jimmy Carter. Carter later introduced ZBB to the national government when he became president. According to Peter Pyhrr, the creator of the ZBB concept, ZBB addresses itself to two basic questions: (1) Are the current activities efficient and effective? (2) Should current activities be eliminated or reduced to fund higher-priority new programs? In addressing these questions, ZBB was said to be able to reduce or eliminate low-priority programs, improve program effectiveness, increase funding to high-impact programs, and retard tax increases.[7]

As with the other rational techniques, ZBB was not a panacea for budgeting. In theory ZBB was radical and could result in great savings. In practice, however, ZBB did not reexamine every item in the budget, as this would require too much organizational upheaval. Many expenditures were mandated by law and therefore were outside the scope of the ZBB process. Because of these factors, ZBB is now more commonly viewed as a marginal than a radical tool of budgeters. The evidence to date indicates that small rather than large changes in budget outputs are likely to occur under ZBB.[8]

On the surface, it originally appeared that agency budget estimates were conforming to ZBB guidelines without the problems of resistance encountered in PBB. In reality, however, major changes in how budgetary decisions were made did not occur. According to Allen Schick, ZBB failed to alter the factors that mattered the most in budgeting. ZBB therefore was said to be a failure in its efforts to produce greater effectiveness.[9]

How might the failure of rational budgeting techniques be explained? One explanation is that budgeting is mainly political and therefore rational techniques cannot be applied. Perhaps in a democracy, issues of efficiency must take a back seat to political concerns. If this is true, then public opinion as well as the actions of powerful interest groups should be viewed as major forces shaping budget priorities. If one accepts this political perspective, then it is advisable for instructors of courses in public budgeting to place less emphasis on disciplines such as economics and finance and focus to a great extent on public relations, opinion shaping, and other factors concerning the "art" of budgeting.

The concept of budgeting as an art rather than a science is not new. V. O. Key, Jr. stated in 1940 that budgeting was actually a matter of value preferences between ends lacking a common denominator. The questions of budgeting, according to Key, should therefore be viewed as a problem of public perception and political philosophy.[10] Key's insights are as relevant today as they were in 1940. The salience of philosophy and political ideology in policymaking must be recognized and understood. This is particularly true when new political philosophies seem to be in great conflict or transition, as occurs today. Results of current conflict in the ideological marketplace of ideas will determine our collective policies and resource priorities. This struggle is of paramount importance and reflects the political or ideological dimensions of budgeting.

Ideology is a real force in the world today, from the Ayatollas in Iran to the so-called Reagan revolution in Washington. This phenomenon of ideological relevance runs counter to the view enunciated by Daniel Bell. In 1960 Bell stated that the age of ideology had ended. This belief was attributed to a perceived consensus that had emerged in the Western world. Acceptance of the welfare state, the desirability of decentralized power, and a system of pluralism were major features of this consensus.[11]

As in the world of Mark Twain, however, Bell's rumors of ideological death were highly exaggerated. The consensus that existed in the 1950s, as reported by Bell, seems to have given way to renewed debate. The size of the welfare state and the desirability of decentralized government are again issues of controversy. The election of Ronald Reagan in 1980 demonstrated that philosophical debate was not dead in the United States and that philosophy could exert great influence in shaping public policy.

Ideology may in fact be superior to the other perspectives

discussed. This ideological perspective is especially relevant when explaining sweeping changes that have occurred over time. According to John Palmer and Isabel Sawhill, the Reagan administration produced great change and was ideological in the sense that it had a clear vision of what it was trying to accomplish. Its objectives were to reduce the size and influence of government, improve national security, restore economic prosperity, and restore traditional values such as work, family, neighborhood, and church.[12]

Basic premises of the Reagan administration's political orientation were that economic growth would flow from the inherent entrepreneurial spirit of Americans, that social problems could be largely solved by institutions such as the family and church, that freedom was our greatest asset, and that freedom required adequate military strength. This coherent belief set provided the philosophical basis for the major redirection of our budgets and our public priorities that occurred in the 1980s.[13]

Given the resurgence of ideology today, its implications and link to public policy must be better understood. Chapter 2 examines the concept of ideology, and Chapter 3 identifies and explains the basic tenets of specific ideologies. This endeavor can help to explain the rationale behind shifts in policy priorities and changes in budget allocations.

NOTES

1. David Ott and Attiat Ott, *Federal Budget Policy* (Washington, D.C.: The Brookings Institution, 1965), p. 43.

2. Morton Halperin, *Bureaucratic Politics and Foreign Policy* (Washington, D.C.: The Brookings Institution, 1974), pp. 56-57.

3. Aaron Wildavsky, "Rescuing Policy Analysis from PPBS," *Public Administration Review* 29 (March/April 1969): 189-202.

4. Allen Schick, "The Road to PPB: The Stages of Budget Reform," *Public Administration Review* 26 (December 1966): 243-58.

5. Quoted in Wildavsky, "Rescuing Policy Analysis from PPBS."

6. Richard Rose, "Implementation and Evaluation: The Record of MBO," in *Contemporary Approaches to Public Budgeting*, ed. F. Kramer (Cambridge, Mass.: Winthrop, 1979).

7. Peter Pyhrr, "The Zero-Base Approach to Government Budgeting," *Public Administration Review* 37 (January/February 1977): 1-8.

8. Allen Schick, "Zero-Base Budgeting and Sunset: Redundancy or Symbiosis?" *The Bureaucrat* 6 (Spring 1977): 12-32.

9. Allen Schick, "The Road from ZBB," *Public Administration Review* 38 (March/April 1978): 177-80.

10. V. O. Key, Jr., "The Lack of a Budgetary Theory," *American Political Science Review* 34 (December 1940): 1137-44.

11. Daniel Bell, *The End of Ideology* (New York: Free Press, 1960), p. 397.

12. John Palmer and Isabel Sawhill, "Overview," in *The Reagan Record*, ed. John Palmer and Isabel Sawhill (Cambridge, Mass.: Ballinger, 1984), p. 2.

13. Ibid.

2

The Concept of Political Ideology

A great deal of confusion and uncertainty surround the concept of ideology. Terms such as "Marxism," "Maoism," "socialism," "conservatism," "liberalism," "fascism," and "libertarianism" are associated with specific belief sets. Understanding of these belief sets is important in both predicting and improving public policies. The study of ideology also helps to identify nonrational dogmatic behavior, behavior that may be less successful in accomplishing concrete objectives than in adhering to a prescribed vision.

In the pure scientific sense, ideologies are concepts. Concepts have been defined as theoretical creations based upon observations but that cannot be observed directly or indirectly.[1] Concepts are much vaguer than things we can feel or touch. Concepts are even more ambiguous than things that we can indirectly identify, such as the sex of a survey respondent identified through a mailed questionnaire. Concepts are sets of mental images that refer to something we wish to define. Liberalism, religiosity, and prejudice are examples of mental images we wish to define. One cannot physically touch liberalism, religiosity, or prejudice, yet one can acquire a general understanding of the meaning of these terms. As Supreme Court Justice Potter Stewart once inferred, one might not be able to define a specific concept such as pornography, but one might feel that one knows it when one sees it.

Earl Babbie suggests that concepts such as prejudice are terms that we have agreed to use in communication that represent a collection of related phenomena.[2] Problems arise with abstract concepts because images of the concept may differ between places, times, or individuals. In order to define ambiguous concepts objectively, specific sets of indicators that identify the concept must be formulated. These indicators must be observable, either directly or indirectly, and can be used to identify the presence or absence of the concept. For example, one might define the concept "conservative" by the following attitudes: desire for an aggressive foreign policy, low taxes, less government intervention in the private sector, less public spending on social programs, greater morality in society, and a fondness for dark blue ties. The term "conservative" could then be systematically identified by its correspondence to these established indicators.

PROBLEMS OF OPERATIONALIZING CONCEPTS

Many problems exist in efforts to operationalize concepts. The first problem is a term's inability consistently to hold its meaning over time. This phenomenon is characterized as the problem of time dimension.

Sometimes labels persist long after the ideas associated with them have faded. For example, the label "liberalism" is still used to classify a specific set of beliefs; however, the beliefs associated with the concept today differ significantly from the beliefs that were associated with the term 200 years ago. Adam Smith, the father of modern capitalism, was considered a classical liberal of the eighteenth century. Liberals of Smith's period strongly supported the concept of limited government as well as the sanctity of private property. These classical liberals also possessed an inherent faith in the value of unrestrained pursuit of individual gains. These values do not correspond to the core positions of politicians who are considered to be liberal in the United States today. These values accurately portray only the views of individuals considered liberal at one point in time—namely, the eighteenth and nineteenth centuries. The previous indicators of liberalism are not associated with its present connotation; thus it suffers from the problem of time dimension identified earlier. These operationalization problems of time dimension are also observable when foreign policies are considered.

Not long ago, conservatives in the United States were associated with policies of isolation whereas liberals advocated more intervention in foreign affairs. World War I occurred during the liberal Democratic administration of Woodrow Wilson, World War II during the liberal administration of Franklin D. Roosevelt, and the Vietnam war during the liberal administration of Lyndon Johnson. Between the first and second world wars, conservative Republican senators such as Henry Lodge blocked efforts to move the United States toward a more interventionist posture. Involvement in the League of Nations was also blocked by conservative legislators who called for less American intervention in foreign affairs. Conservative Republican presidents such as Warren Harding and Calvin Coolidge advocated nonintervention in foreign affairs and a "return to normalcy" after the disruption of World War I.

Today conservative politicians in the United States, such as Ronald Reagan, Alexander Haig, and Jack Kemp, are considered much more interventionist than liberal politicians. This represents a reversal of roles from the post-World War I period when conservative senators rejected the interventionist philosophies of liberals such as Woodrow Wilson.

Another example of the time dimension problem is viewed in changes that have occurred with popular labels. Labels remain the same, but the images associated with those labels can change drastically. In the 1950s, products with the label "made in Japan" inferred low price and inferior quality. This, as we all know, is no longer the case. Today's Japanese radios, stereos, televisions, microwave ovens, and automobiles are actually preferred by large numbers of Americans and are more expensive than comparable U.S. products. As with the conception of liberalism, great changes in our perception of the label "made in Japan" have occurred. This changing perception has been rather dramatic and has occurred in a relatively short time span. It represents a good example of how mental images may be altered over time and how new perceptions eventually replace the older views that no longer hold true. As a corollary to the label "made in Japan," the label "made in the U.S.A." no longer connotes the image of quality that it once possessed.

A second problem that exists in operationalizing concepts is that of label variance. This refers to the extent to which variation exists with the images associated with a term. At any one time a wide range of images may be linked to the same term. For example, the concept "Democratic party ideology" conjures up not one but a wide variety of images. The philosophy of the Democratic party is not monolithic or cohesive.

The liberal organization Americans for Democratic Action (ADA) assesses the political perspectives of legislators in the U.S. Congress and arrays them on the "liberal" to "conservative" continuum. The ADA evaluates how liberal or how conservative a legislator is on the basis of votes he or she makes for or against specific bills. Using these evaluations, philosophical variation within the Democratic party is found to be massive, ranging from the conservative views of members such as Sonny Montgomery of Mississippi, Larry McDonald of Georgia, and Bill Nichols of Alabama (all with 1982 ADA ratings of 5) to the liberal views of members such as Thomas Downey of New York, Don Edwards of California, and

Edward Markey of Massachusetts (all with 1982 ADA ratings of 100).

The greater the degree of variance or disagreement with regard to what a concept such as "Democratic party ideology" stands for, the weaker the usefulness of the concept. If people cannot agree on specific components of a concept, it will have little value in research and little generalizability. Because of the huge variation in views that exists among members of the Democratic party, the concept "Democratic party ideology" would be exceptionally difficult to operationalize and its research value would be very limited. The problem that exists with label variance is the question of how one identifies something if there is no agreement in regard to its composition. As with the blind men and the elephant, each individual might have a different idea about the ultimate composition of the entity.

A final problem that exists in the conceptualization of concepts is that of frame of reference. Terms may mean different things to different people. This is not attributed to variation within the term itself (such as in the term "Democratic party ideology"), nor is it attributable to changes in the term over time. Frame of reference problems arise from the fact that individuals can view terms from totally different perspectives. For example, to a beatnik of the 1950s, the term "cool" signified something quite different from a weatherman's definition on the 6 o'clock news. To a hippie of the 1960s, the term "far out" conjured up images different from those of an astronomer. To a follower of the Ayatollah Khomenei in the 1980s, the term "religious fundamentalism" implies something quite different from what it means to the followers of Billy Graham. Frame of reference therefore can lead to great confusion and must be clarified when discussing ideological concepts. Each of these problems (time dimension, label variance, and frame of reference) contributes to the confusion that surrounds the concept of ideology.

IDEOLOGY DEFINED

Numerous definitions of ideology abound, but, as with the term "pornography," a definitive understanding of the concept remains elusive. Historically, the term "ideology" is traceable to the time of the French Revolution. It originated with the Institut de France, an association of intellectuals created around the time of the revolution. The members of the Institut de France were unique; they were said to value freedom of thought above other considerations, such as the pursuit of material rewards. Ideology was therefore said to represent a novel science of ideas. To French Institute members such as Antoine Destutt de Tracy (1754–1836), ideology was the source of enlightened policies that would contribute to political stability. Ideology was said to refer to a new "value-free" source of knowledge that was to lead postrevolutionary France. Through the use of reason, this new science was believed capable of shaping society for the common good.[3]

Ideology or the philosophy of reason, however, was not to be the major factor shaping postrevolutionary France. Napoleon was critical of "ideologues," claiming that they were dreamers divorced from reality. Napoleon contended that members of the institute could not adapt their ideas to the practical situations of real life. In order to establish a strong central state, he decided to throw his support to the Church rather than support the ambiguous new "science of ideas."[4]

The concept of ideology as we know it relates more to the work of George Hegel and Karl Marx than to the early French philosophers. To Hegel, ideology was less a "science of ideas" than a means of explaining history. Hegel maintained that men were merely instruments of history and, furthermore, that these men as instruments of history acted with "imperfect consciousness." Given that the true meaning of history was said to be concealed, men could act irrationally. History in contrast to the individual action of men was thought to be logical and could be explained by a mechanism termed the "dialectical process." In this dialectical process, conflict between existing ideas and new ideas results in a synthesis of the best elements of both. Good ideas are therefore never lost in the process but help to form a more complete whole.

Marx borrowed extensively from the ideas of Hegel. Great similarities exist in a number of their basic concepts. To Hegel, ideology represented the "imperfect consciousness" of man; to Marx, ideology referred to "false consciousness" or mistaken beliefs about society shared by the whole community. Illusions common to nearly all persons in a society were said to be produced by ruling groups in order to maintain control.

In the theories of both Marx and Hegel, ideology referred to the inability of individuals to understand the true meaning of their actions. Marx believed that ideology was linked to ideas and interests of a particular group or social class. Ideology, according to his interpretation, referred to distorted rationalizations that were indoctrinated into the exploited masses by the ruling interests of society. Ideology, according to Marx, was less a "science of ideas" than the means by which the dominant economic interests justified their control over others.

Other social scientists further refined the conception of ideology developed by Hegel and Marx. Karl Mannheim was one of these theorists. Mannheim believed that the term "ideology" should be dichotomized into two distinct components: the particular conception of ideology and the total conception of ideology.[5] To Mannheim, the particular conception referred to skepticism about the ideas advanced by one's opponent, whereas the total conception of ideology was much broader, referring to the dominant thoughts of an age or the dominant thoughts of a group within a given age. Utilizing this broad conception of ideology, Mannheim believed that one could not compare isolated thoughts from one age to another but must strive to understand the thought system within the context in which the thought was developed.

The concept of ideology is important to philosophers and students of epistemology, which refers to the development of knowledge. Ideologies can also be perceived as having practical value. They can help to explain the advancement or curtailment of specific public policies. They can help to explain policy conflicts between adversarial groups in society. They can help to explain the differing perspectives between competing groups in our pluralistic society. The concept of ideology developed by Hegel, Marx, and Mannheim helps to explain why different individuals have different perceptions of the world and why individuals ascribing to different belief sets or ideologies are unable to agree with one another. Reo Christenson claimed that ideology polarizes antagonistic groups and creates "we–they" types of characterizations. For example, ideology creates a scenario in which one group asserts that it has great leaders while the opposing group has tyrants, one group is true to its principles while the opposing group is fanatical, one group has a just political philosophy while the other group is composed of misguided ideologues.[6]

Ideology as we know it also is moralistic and dramatic. Lewis Feuer maintained that ideology gives meaning to the lives of intellectuals of a society's younger generation by following, in some fashion, the Mosaic myth. Feuer defines the Mosaic myth by the following scenario: A people are oppressed. A young man, not himself of the oppressed, appears. Moved by sympathy, he strikes down the oppressor's henchman and flees. He experiences the call to redeem the oppressed and returns to demand freedom for the oppressed. He is spurned by the ruler. He leads action that, after initial defeat, overwhelms the oppressor. He liberates the oppressed people. After liberation, the young man imparts a new law to his people. The newly liberated people relapse from loyalty to their historic mission. The leader imposes a collective discipline on the people. A false prophet arises who rebels against the leader's authoritative rule but is destroyed. The leader, now the revered lawgiver, dies as he glimpses from afar the new existence.[7]

A number of contemporary authors have also attempted to define ideology. Many define ideology in terms of ideas that provide a set of political beliefs and values that are coherently integrated. Everett Ladd believed that "like a quilt, an ideology is more than the sum of its patches; it is patches bound together in a specified and ordered arrangement that isn't just a random collection of beliefs but rather a coherent view of the world."[8] Furthermore, Ladd contended that ideology provides answers to such questions as how government should be organized, how power should be distributed, and what political values the society should try to realize.[9] Austin Ranney defined ideology as "a relatively comprehensive and explicit system of cognitive and moral beliefs about people and society that constitutes the basis for a political program or system."[10] L. T. Sargent stated that ideologies are composed of sets of attitudes toward various institutions and processes of society. They provide the believer with a picture of the world both as it is and as it should be. Ideologies are also said to organize the tremendous complexity of the world into something fairly simple and understandable.[11] Kenneth Hoover defined ideology as ideas about how power in society should be organized.[12] This is consistent with Ladd's conception as well as that of Marx.

Ideologies are said to reflect some assessments of the power relationships that exist in society. Ideologies often represent militant and revolutionary ideas that oppose the status quo.[13] These revolutionary ideas often consist of an assessment of the status quo and a vision of the future that is materially better than that of the present.[14] Ideology has also been viewed as ideals, morals, and rationalizations that serve the interests of a ruling class.[15] Although there is no single universally accepted definition of ideology, most authors believe its importance is unquestionable.

WHY STUDY IDEOLOGY?

The study of ideology is pursued for multiple objectives. From a purely academic point of view, one can study ideology to gain knowledge simply for its own sake. From a political activist's point of view, one might want to study ideology to buttress political positions and to learn the weaknesses of philosophical enemies. From an administrative point of view, an understanding of ideology can help in the neutral assessment of public policies. Policy evaluation and creation will improve if rigid interpretation of dogma can be identified, controlled, and replaced with more neutral analysis. In this regard ideology can be utilized to come full circle back to the goals of a "value-free" science of knowledge enunciated by Antoine Destutt de Tracy and the members of the Institut de France.

Investigation of philosophical predispositions should be a starting point in the identification of biases. Policy analysts can then attempt to mitigate the more egregious excesses of ideologically biased policy. More efficient and effective public policy will result from these efforts. If a value-free science is indeed possible, ideological biases must be exposed and eliminated.

In the United States, differences in philosophical perspective are evident between individuals characterized as "liberals" and those identified as "conservatives." Philosophical perspectives between individuals, however, may be more likely to differ in terms of means than ends. In a broad sense, both liberals and conservatives probably agree that security, prosperity, and opportunity are desirable ends for society. Conservatives and liberals, however, are likely to differ in regard to the appropriate means of reaching those desirable ends. For example, one group may seek to ensure security through longer prison sentences, whereas another group may want to ensure security through providing more jobs and opportunities to the poor.

If agreement is reached in terms of ends for society, it is conceivable that the effectiveness of various means for reaching those ends can be empirically tested. Research designs could effectively measure the extent of goal attainment when various strategies and policies are implemented. Unfortunately, the ability of social scientists to conduct neutral and objective policy evaluation is suspect. One factor contributing to this failure within the discipline is the philosophical or ideological biases of analysts. Intersubjectivity in social science analysis is given lip service as a desired end, but it is an end that is yet to be realized. A fuller understanding of the ideological underpinnings of policy may help to reduce this problem of bias arising from philosophical perceptions.

Ideologies help analysts to understand and evaluate policy by explaining intellectual themes of our society. Kenneth Hoover stated that political ideologies form a language of justification for public policy decisions affecting people's lives. He expressed no doubt that actions were linked to ideas.[16] It is clear that societies have been reshaped, sacrifices made, and wars fought over ideas and the more complete ideologies that have developed over time. Ideas have influenced broad global conflicts as well as more narrowly defined questions. Chapter 3 reviews major political ideologies in an effort to gain a greater understanding of what specific ideologies represent and an idea of how they may influence policy. It is hoped that if ideologies are better understood, they can be controlled, leading to greater rationality and objectivity in the development of public policy. Through a greater understanding of these ideologies it is also hoped that public administrators will be better equipped to identify biases, test the effects of those biases, and ultimately produce more effective policy decisions.

NOTES

1. Earl Babbie, *The Practice of Social Research* (Belmont, Calif.: Wadsworth, 1983), p. 105.

2. Ibid.

3. Robert Eccleshall, Vincent Geoghegan, Richard Jay, and Rick Wilford, *Political Ideologies* (London: Hutchinson and Company, 1984), p. 25.

4. A. M. Drucker, *The Political Uses of Ideology* (New York: Harper & Row, 1974), p. 13.

5. Karl Mannheim, *Ideology and Utopia* (London: Routledge & Kegan Paul, 1936), p. 49.

6. Reo Christenson, Alan Engel, Dan Jacobs, Mostafa Rejai, and Herbert Waltzer, *Ideologies and Modern Politics* (London: Thomas Nelson & Sons, 1971), p. 2.

7. Lewis Feuer, *Ideology and the Ideologists* (Oxford: Basil Blackwell, 1975).

8. Everett C. Ladd, *The American Polity* (New York: W. W. Norton, 1987), p. 58.

9. Ibid.

10. Austin Ranney, *Governing* (Englewood Cliffs, N.J.: Prentice-Hall, 1987), p. 165.

11. Lyman T. Sargent, *Contemporary Political Ideologies* (Homewood, Ill.: The Dorsey Press, 1981), p. 1.

12. Kenneth Hoover, *Ideology and Political Life* (Monterey, Calif.: Brooks/Cole, 1986), p. 4.

13. Frederick Watkins, *The Age of Ideology—Political Thought, 1950 to the Present* (Englewood Cliffs, N.J.: Prentice-Hall, 1964).

14. David Ingersoll, *Communism, Fascism, and Democracy* (Columbus, Oh.: Charles E. Merrill, 1971).

15. Paul Sweezy, "Vietnam: Endless War," in *The Failure of American Liberalism*, ed. Marvin Gottleman and David Mermelstein (New York: Vintage Books, 1970), p. 594.

16. Hoover, *Ideology and Political Life*, p. 5.

3

Specific Ideologies: Nationalism, Communism, Socialism, Capitalism, Fascism, and Democracy

In a broad sense, ideology represents views of the world that are internally consistent and held by a large number of people. An ideology differs from an individual's belief in that an ideology provides the follower with a comprehensive and understandable view of the world. Ideologies also supply followers with an assessment of the world from a particular perspective and a normative prescription of what is necessary in order to improve life.

Most Americans would not be considered ideologues because they do not ascribe to rigid sets of beliefs to explain behavior taking place in the world. Americans are more likely to be characterized as pragmatists. Nevertheless, Americans are still influenced by an array of belief systems. These different systems act to shape public opinion and public policy. Some of these systems are described in this chapter to provide insight into the philosophical bases of public policies.

NATIONALISM

A major ideology, again, represents a belief system that is internally consistent and accepted as true by a large number of people. Lyman Sargent stated that every ideology of the twentieth century has at some time been affected by nationalism.[1] Nationalism is expressed in the emotion that binds people in a community. The outer manifestations of nationalism are observable through tangible symbols, such as a nation's flag or a country's national anthem. Nationalism deals with the recognition that our lives are wrapped up in the lives of others and are often laden with emotion.

Nationalism can be viewed as a manner in which individuals identify with groups. Location is usually associated with this group identification. Either by birth or by long-term association, a place becomes important. Through this process, residents of locations resent criticism of their homeland and become part of the larger whole. A national consciousness or national identity develops that contributes greatly to the development of patriotism and nationalism.

Sargent believed that the term "patriotism" as commonly used can best be defined as love of country. When it is said that some people are patriotic, it is implied that those people are aware of being part of a larger group, that they identify with that group and have positive feelings toward it. In common usage, "nationalism" is synonymous with "patriotism" except that it also refers to demands made and actions taken in addition to mere feelings.[2]

Leon Baradat recognized the tremendous influence of the concept of nationalism. Baradat stated that nationalism was the most powerful political idea of the past several hundred years. Nationalism, or the idea of the nation-state, was claimed to be so powerful that it dominated every other idea system. To Baradat, nationalism creates a mirror in which individuals observe, assess, and react to events. Nationalism was perceived to be so powerful that it was viewed as beyond reason, rooted in irrationalism, given that the commitment demanded by it was almost completely emotional. It sometimes required its followers to sacrifice family, fortune, and even life itself for the good of the state. Nationalism also established artificial barriers between people by producing identification based on geographic territory.[3]

A standard definition of nationalism mentions feelings of national consciousness, exaltation of one nation over others, loyalty, and the promotion of culture.[4] Nationalism can be associated with movements within a larger political entity. Examples of this are Black Nationalists in the United States, Basques in Spain, and French-Canadian separatists in Quebec. Nationalism is also associated with such diverse behavior as anti-imperialism in the Third World and aggressive expansionism of developed countries.

Justification for nationalism is found in both liberal and conservative philosophies. Nationalism was a progressive doctrine in the late eighteenth and early nineteenth centuries. It was a focal point for opposition to oppressive regimes and foreign control. The French Revolution not only had the effect of destroying the traditional aristocracy, it also created a sense of national responsibility in citizens by demanding a sense of loyalty and devotion to the state.

Nationalism has been studied from two different perspectives: liberal nationalism and right-wing nationalism. Liberal nationalism was opposed to the authoritarian politics of the nineteenth century. It reflected democratic ideas and was associated with the ideal of social progress. Giuseppe Mazzini (1805–72) embodied liberal nationalism through his love of humanity, belief in popular sovereignty, Italian patriotism, and the view that national self-determination could bring peace, prosperity, and freedom to Europe. Mazzini founded the Young Italy and Young Europe movements in an effort to overthrow oppressive conservative political regimes that tended to dominate in Europe during his lifetime.

Right-wing nationalism emerged in the latter part of the nineteenth century. Liberal nationalism was replaced by militarism, suspicion of foreign nations, protectionism, and the suppression of opposition. German nationalism arose largely as a reaction to the encroaching French culture. German philosophers such as Johann Fichte (1762–1814) argued that the distinct culture expressed through the German language could be preserved only by unification of those who spoke the language within a state. After French armies defeated Austria and Prussia in 1807, philosophers such as Fichte advocated the creation of a state based on German culture that could match the power of the French state. Fulfillment of this vision came with the victory of Prussia over France in 1870 and the unification of Germany.

Nationalism remains a force that transcends other ideologies. It can be applied to explain numerous historical conflicts such as World Wars I and II, conflict between Polish trade union movements and the Soviet Union, as well as conflicts between Palestinians and Israelis. Transnational organizations such as the United Nations, the Organization of Petroleum-Exporting Countries, the North Atlantic Treaty Organization, and the European Community have been created in efforts to foster greater unity and overcome barriers of nationalism. Most observers, however, are highly skeptical of the likelihood that these transnational organizations could replace nation-states as centers of political and cultural identification.

COMMUNISM

The term "communism" evokes numerous images in contemporary American society. Communism to some is merely an excuse for totalitarian rule, a threat to capitalist values, and the enemy of Western society in general. Others view communism as a theory that has yet to be successfully implemented. According to the latter theory, a more humane and equitable world can be created. Communist philosophy is heavily influenced by the ideas of Karl Marx and Vladimir Lenin.

A common definition of communism is that it represents a theory advocating the elimination of private property. Furthermore, it reflects a system in which goods are owned commonly rather than privately and a system in which goods are available to each according to his or her needs. Perhaps the best way to gain an understanding of communist ideology is to review the major theories developed by Marx and Lenin.

Karl Marx (1818–83) developed a number of concepts that are widely accepted today by millions of followers. Among the more important concepts developed by Marx in his very extensive writings are the following.[5]

1. *Alienation.* Marx believed that under the system of capitalism, individuals are cut off from themselves, their families, and their work. They cannot become fully developed human beings in this type of system. Individuals are said to be alienated from the activities of their own labor because they are forced to work against their wishes. Forced labor is said to be dehumanizing and against human nature. Workers are also viewed as alienated from the products of their labor because the products are not the result of their own creativity but the results of involuntary activities. The product of labor is said to produce alienation because it does not belong to the workers but to the capitalist who owns the means of production.

2. *Dialectical materialism.* Marx believed that a basic tool of analysis is the dialectical process. The dialectic is believed to have originated in ancient Greece and describes a means of attaining truth through a process of questions and answers. Hegel refined the concept, maintaining that ideas develop through the process of thesis (established idea), antithesis (conflicting idea), and synthesis (a combination of the two thoughts). Synthesis is said to represent the best elements of the thesis and antithesis; it becomes the established idea, and the process repeats itself.

3. *Class structure.* Marx believed that the division of labor in all societies leads to the development of a class structure. The different classes were established according to their relationship to the means of production. The ruling class was said

to be the "capitalists," who had control of the means of production. All other classes were subordinate to this group.

4. *False consciousness*. This refers to people's false impression of the relationships that exist in society. According to Marx, people falsely believe that they are masters of their own fate while they are really subject to forces of history. False consciousness prevents people from seeing the true relationships among classes that exist in society and prevents them from seeing the exploitation that occurs between economic groups.

5. *Surplus value*. According to Marx's labor theory of value, the value of a commodity is equal to the average number of hours needed to produce the product. The owner of the means of production, however, pays the worker less than the labor value of the commodity produced. The difference between the full value of a commodity and the amount paid the worker is considered profit or, in Marx's terminology, surplus value. Surplus value is therefore said to be produced by the worker and appropriated by the capitalist.

6. *Revolution*. Class struggle in capitalist countries would ultimately end in a revolutionary victory of the working class over the owners of the means of production. Workers would revolt when they became aware of their common interest in ending the exploitative rule of the capitalists. Revolution is believed to be necessary for meaningful change to occur given that no ruling class would voluntarily give up its power. Violence is condoned because it ultimately will lead to a more equitable society in which the masses would benefit. A dictatorship of the workers would be set up for a brief period as a transitional stage leading to a better society.

7. *Capitalism*. Capitalism is viewed as a mode of production that brings misery, chaos, and crisis to society. Capitalism forces individuals to sell their human labor power as commodities, therefore degrading and alienating themselves. Capitalism is viewed as a system that accumulates resources and forces investment of resources at a constantly falling rate of

profit. Competition bankrupts all but the small number of successful entrepreneurs while at the same time increasing the number of people who belong to the working class. As the members of the working class increase, they compete and wages fall. Capitalism is believed ultimately to produce a situation in which there is excess productive capacity, a surplus of unemployed workers, a surplus of commodities that cannot be sold, and increased misery. Marx predicted that capitalism would collapse and then workers would be able to reorganize the economy in order to terminate exploitation and inequality.

Vladimir Lenin adopted the philosophy of Marx and transformed it into a hybrid philosophy called Marxist-Leninism. Important concepts developed by Lenin are described below.[6]

1. *Professional revolutionary.* Marx maintained that the working class would develop its own leader as well as a class consciousness. Lenin believed that small groups of professional revolutionaries were necessary because the masses were incapable of self-emancipation. The masses would become instruments in the hands of an elite of professional revolutionaries. Lenin advised "professional revolutionaries" to organize into small groups or cells and infiltrate established institutions such as schools, churches, labor unions, and political parties.

2. *Party.* The revolutionary party was required to be an elitist organization, highly disciplined and secret in character. The party would consist of the best-qualified professional revolutionaries, who would act as the vanguard or advance guard of the workers. The party would express for the workers what they truly felt but were incapable of expressing themselves. The party was said to be the repository of consciousness, would govern for the good of the people, but would not be governed by the people. Once policy was established, the party had to be sure that the rank and file of the working class acted according to party commands.

3. *Democratic centralism.* This organizational device combines freedom of discussion with centralized control. Before

any decision is made by the party, there should be complete freedom to dissent. After the decision has been made, however, it must be accepted unanimously. Once members have had an opportunity to speak, all dissent is to be suppressed. This was justified by the view that a party committed to a course of action could not tolerate dissenters within its ranks.

4. *Imperialism*. This concept purports to explain why revolution occurs in less-developed countries. The theory maintains that capitalism has found a way out of its problems through the use of cheap labor and cheap raw materials taken from underdeveloped countries. World society is seen as being divided into two camps: the exploiters and the exploited. Revolution in the colonial world aims to destroy imperialism and the capitalist system that it represents.

The philosophy of communism is complex and distinct from the philosophy of socialism. Jean-François Revel stated that communism was really an enemy of socialism and a traitor to many of its lofty ideals. He claimed that communism represented a "totalitarian temptation" and was the greatest danger facing mankind today. Revel felt that communism was an adversary of socialism because it gave birth to the most powerful nation-states the world has ever known and because it uses themes of socialism in propagating its own expansion. Communism exploits the discontent that is present in capitalism. It destroys political democracy in the name of socialism and is said thereafter to install a political order that is neither democratic nor socialist. It is in terms of economic performance and respect for human rights, in the opinion of Revel, vastly inferior to capitalism.[7]

SOCIALISM

Modern socialism emerged as a response to the vast industrial and social changes of the nineteenth century. Socialists were critical of the new industrial society that was developing and believed in common rather than private ownership of the means of production. Socialists focused upon the cooperative element in human nature in contrast to the individualistic profit motive that is essential to the theory of capitalism. Socialists advocated equality in place of competition. A socialist party would not produce winners and losers in a competitive game with the object of accumulating wealth. The unequal distribution of wealth that arose from this pursuit was said to be a hallmark of capitalist society.

Socialism is in fundamental disagreement with capitalism in regard to its perspective of the best method to bring about maximum welfare for people in society. Capitalism exalts the virtues of individual property and incentive, whereas socialism focuses on the benefits of collective effort. Collectivization and anti-individualism are characteristics of socialist as well as communist thought. Socialism shares similarities with communism, yet many significant differences remain. William Ebenstein described the following differences between the philosophies of socialism and communism.[8]

1. Communists seek to bring about the end of capitalism by a single act of revolutionary upheaval and civil war. Socialists adhere to strict constitutional procedures, seeking power by ballot rather than bullets.

2. Communists visualize the transition from capitalist enterprise to public ownership as sudden and complete. Socialists believe that public ownership of the means of production is to be built gradually.

3. Communists insist on total nationalization because they believe that publicly owned property is always preferable to private enterprise. Socialists identify particular instances when a specific industry or service is to be transferred to public ownership and control.

4. Communism reflected in Lenin's theory of the professional revolutionary is based on the assumption that the majority of the people are unable to think for themselves, that the party must lead, and that within the party a small group of people are able to formulate policy. This elite concept is rejected by socialists, who believe in democracy and majority rule.

5. Communists feel that it is useless to seek change by persuasion considering that all means of communication, education, and propaganda are biased in favor of the capitalist status quo. Socialists believe in peaceful persuasion as the only method of promoting their program.

6. Communists believe that every capitalist system is a dictatorship. Democratic institutions in a capitalist system are considered to be a facade. Democratic institutions are also considered to be hypocritical. Socialists draw a fundamental distinction between two types of capitalist system, the political dictatorship and the liberal democracy.

7. Communists maintain that the choice in a democracy is between full capitalism and full collectivism. Socialists see the transition from a predominantly capitalist economy to a predominantly socialist economy as gradual.

8. Communists think in terms of three absolutes: capitalism, revolution, and communist dictatorship. Socialists think in terms of three relative stages: a predominantly capitalist economy, a long-term gradual change, and finally a predominantly socialized economy.

Socialism as a political philosophy should not be confused with Marxist-Leninism or Soviet imperialism. Joseph Schumpeter wrote in 1946 that the trouble with the Soviet Union is not that it is socialist but that it is nationalistic and imperialistic. He felt that the Soviet regime was essentially a military aristocracy that, ruled by means of a strictly disciplined party, did not allow freedom of the press, and in reality exploited the masses.[9]

Comparing socialism with communism identifies differences between these two ideologies; however it does not provide a clear definition of either system. Sidney Hook helps to accomplish this task by enumerating a number of facets of socialism. First, socialism believes in the value of public ownership of the means of production. Nationalization would end unemployment because production (aimed at addressing the needs of society) theoretically would keep going as long as social needs existed. The evils of the business cycle would be avoided in socialism because industry would operate with the public good in mind rather than operate only for profit and hard cash.[10]

Under the socialist vision, planning would enable managers to eliminate the duplication and waste found in the capitalist system. Socialism would emphasize human welfare and social justice. In a socialist society opportunities would exist for all. Every individual would be able to mature and develop an independent and harmonious personality. Individuals would be able to make meaningful use of leisure, there would be revulsion against monetary values, and people would find real worth in others, in art, religion, and science.[11]

According to Leon Baradat, there are three features of socialism: (1) ownership of production, (2) the welfare state, and (3) socialist intent. Socialist intent is perceived to be the most essential element and promotes the goal of setting people free from the condition of material dependence. Socialism, however, is said to go beyond redistribution of wealth. It foresees a new relationship among individuals based on a plentiful supply of goods. Its goal is to establish a completely new social order in which human cooperation is the basis of action.[12]

CAPITALISM

The philosophy of capitalism has been both denounced as the scourge of humanity and praised as the salvation of humanity. Which of these perspectives is closer to the truth is a matter of personal preference. Irving Kristol maintained that capitalism in the United States has a historical legitimacy that is not present anywhere else in the world. Kristol stated that the United States is the capitalist nation par excellence because the Founding Fathers regarded capitalism as the only set of economic arrangements consistent with the liberal democracy they had established.[13] In order to understand more fully the philosophy of liberalism and its place in American society, it is first necessary to review the thoughts of

Adam Smith, the great Scottish philosopher, viewed by many as the intellectual father of capitalism.

In *Wealth of Nations*, Smith argued that the wealth of a nation and the best interests of individuals in the nation could be maximized if individuals were allowed to pursue their self-interests without governmental interference.[14] Government in 1776 (the time Smith published *Wealth of Nations*) was perceived to be the enemy of liberty because of restrictive laws that limited the freedom of workers and hampered free exchange in foreign markets. This interference by government into the marketplace was believed to prevent the most efficient use of resources and therefore produced negative consequences for both the individual and society.

Ownership of property on an individual rather than a collective basis was advocated for a number of reasons. First, power would be diffused among many separate individuals rather than concentrated. Second, a free market system based on private property and incentive was believed to be more productive and efficient. Major principles developed by Adam Smith in his theory of capitalism follow.

1. *Individual freedom.* According to this principle, free individuals do not intend to promote the public interest but, if left free, will direct their interest to the greatest value. This is done for selfish reasons; yet in promoting their own gain, they are guided by an "invisible hand" that promotes the good of all. Society in general is thought to be more prosperous and efficient when it allows individuals to have greater freedom. Society in general is perceived as less prosperous when it enforces tight regulations characteristic of the earlier mercantilist era. Individuals are believed to be better able to judge their most profitable use than the state. Given that the wealth of the nation is the aggregate of individual wealth of members in society, the wealth of the nation is maximized by leaving individuals alone to pursue their own interests. This view lies at the very heart of the concept of capitalism and provides a major distinction between free and planned societies.

2. *Role of government*. Smith did not advocate the absence of government but believed in a limited role for the public sector. In one sense Smith can be viewed as an early advocate of "getting government off the backs of the people." Smith stated that the government had only three legitimate duties to attend to: (1) protecting society from violence and invasion from other nations, (2) administration of justice, and (3) erecting and maintaining public works that would not have great value to any individual but would benefit society. According to Smith, an interventionist government would probably be inefficient because it could hinder the flow of activity to areas of greatest opportunity and greatest want. As stated previously, individuals acting alone are said to be the best determinant of their own actions. Freedom for individual action and decision making therefore is a fundamental principle that ensures the maximum economic well-being for society.

Smith advocated a small government entity because in a society of limited governmental control, individuals would be better able to act in their own self-interests to maximize their wealth. Individual producers would be free to seek profit, consumers would be free to buy the goods they desired, and workers would be free to seek the highest wages for their services. Smith believed that in order to ensure maximum prosperity for a society, government should not interfere with these freedoms.

3. *Self-adjusting market*. Smith believed that every commodity had a "natural" price. The natural price for a commodity depended upon its cost of production or the amount of money paid for wages, rent, and profit in producing the product. When the market price for a commodity was greater than its natural price, more of that commodity would be produced and the market price would sink. When the market price for a commodity was lower than the natural price, production would fall and the market price would rise. This process is also explained in the law of supply and demand. The law of supply and demand demonstrates that production is

not rigid but automatically responds to forces of demand. The law of supply and demand also ensures that reasonable price levels are attained in the marketplace. If demand is high, competition among sellers would drive prices down to the lowest possible level consistent with production. When demand was high, the prospect for profit would ensure that resources would be used to satisfy consumer wants. This would occur through the creation of new businesses to meet the consumer's demand.

Individual freedom is viewed as a mandatory condition for the efficient functioning of this "unfettered" market system. Impediments to competition, such as monopolies and quotas, are said to result in lower levels of economic efficiency and corresponding lower levels in the standard of living.

4. *Private property*. The attainment of private property is an important incentive for people in a competitive society. Psychologically, ownership of property brings a sense of fulfillment, of security, pride, and respect for the property of others. Because profits from private property go directly to the owner, there would be greater incentive to be efficient than would be the case when production goes to a collective agency and is redistributed at a later time according to need.

5. *The profit motive*. The profit motive is an essential element of the free market system for three basic reasons: (1) Profit ensures that producers will be responsive to consumer demand. Consumer tastes change over time, and their new demands will be met because profit is linked to the satisfaction of those desires. Firms that can quickly identify consumer demands and efficiently satisfy those demands will be handsomely rewarded in the form of profit. The consumer is viewed to benefit as well as the producer in this arrangement. (2) Risk taking is rewarded. Society progresses and innovation results from technologically risky ventures. Venture capital is raised and entrepreneurs attempt to carve out a niche in the market. New ventures may lead to higher standards of living through improvements in productivity. (3) Profit

rewards the efficient management of resources. Under free market conditions wasteful companies cannot be profitable over the long term. The most efficient organizations will survive and eventually prosper while the less efficient are forced out of the market.

6. *Competition*. Competition is perhaps the most essential element of capitalist society. Ernest Mandel stated that without competition there would be no capitalist society because there would not be an economic motive to accumulate capital or acquire wealth.[15] Competition is essential in capitalist society in order to ensure efficiency, keep profits down, and duly reward the efficient.

Perhaps the best-known advocate of capitalism today is the conservative economist Milton Friedman. Friedman maintains that economic freedom is a necessary condition for political freedom and that the economic miracle of the United States was made possible by the theories of Adam Smith. Friedman contends that when immigrants came to America, they did not find streets paved with gold, but they did find freedom and an opportunity to make the most of their talents. Through hard work, ingenuity, thrift, and luck, most of them succeeded in realizing enough of their dreams to encourage friends and relatives to join them.[16]

FASCISM

Fascism is regarded by many analysts as a twentieth-century doctrine that began in the 1920s and ended in the 1940s. This perception links the doctrine of fascism to the regimes of Benito Mussolini and Adolf Hitler. "Fascism" is also used to describe any politically conservative or right-wing totalitarian regime. In order to grasp the theoretical basis of fascism, principles of thought predominant in Mussolini's Italy and Hitler's Germany will be described. Technically, only Mussolini's regime (1922–45) was viewed as purely fascist; Hitler's regime (1933–45) was considered a combination of different philosophies and termed National Socialist. Many analysts believe that although differences existed between the two regimes, they were similar enough to be combined into one ideology. Key elements of the fascist ideology developed by both Mussolini and Hitler are therefore discussed.[17]

1. *Irrationalism*. Fascism and National Socialism rejected the application of reason and science to the solution of social problems. The basic assumptions of these systems were that people are not rational, they need not be reasoned with, and they can be manipulated. Use of myth and appeals to emotion were believed effective in manipulating the masses. Life, according to the fascist ideology, defied rational explanation. Because irrationality ruled, it was believed that policy was molded by instinct and emotion. These ideas of irrationalism were derived largely from the writings of French author Georges Sorel and German philosopher Arthur Schopenhauer. Sorel stressed the importance of propagating a myth in order to accomplish one's objectives. The myth, according to Sorel, need not have foundation in reality but must be present for the sake of creating an emotional force that could mobilize the masses to action. Schopenhauer believed that life was the product of uncontrollable impulsive action. He termed this impulse "the will" and stated that it was blind, erratic, and unpredictable. Schopenhauer concluded that rational explanations of life are meaningless because the will is a force without justification. People have no alternative but to submit to the will.

2. *Nationalism and the state*. Both Mussolini and Hitler attempted to unite the people of their nations under nationalist banners. In Italy, Mussolini sought to revive the glory of ancient Rome. In Germany, Hitler sought national unity and aggrandizement through appeals to racism. Mussolini believed that individuals must give all of their loyalty, dedication, and love to the nation. To Hitler, nationalism was integrally tied to racism. The German nation would be advanced by stressing the importance of the German race and Nordic values. The

state or German nation would be developed in such a manner that it would monopolize all power and authority. It would control everything in society including the economy, industry, labor, family, school, church, and peer groups. George Orwell's vision in his classic book *1984* is an example of this type of society in which individual freedom is replaced by total submission to the state.

3. *Racism*. This is a dominant theme of German fascism. The writings of the French author Arthur de Gobineau (1816–82) and English author Houston Chamberlain (1855–1927) greatly influenced the development of racist thought. Gobineau maintained that the Aryan race was superior to all other races. At various times the Aryans were said to have imposed their will on inferior races but through intermarriage their civilization eventually declined. Gobineau stated that the Aryan race remained somewhat pure in Ireland, England, northern France, the Benelux countries, and Scandinavia. The German people were believed to be the least racially mixed, giving them a genetic advantage over all others in fostering the next advanced civilization. Chamberlain contended that the Aryan race had created all the world's civilizations but that these civilizations declined as a result of impurity produced by intermarriage. Chamberlain argued that good was personified in the Aryan people, particularly Germans, who were the purest race. Evil was personified by inferior races, and history was viewed as a struggle between Aryan good and evil propagated by inferior races.

Also influential in the development of theories of race was Friedrich Nietzsche (1844–1900). Nietzsche referred to the idea of the will developed by Schopenhauer. To Nietzsche, however, the will had meaning as a force that stimulated people to engage in combat and dominate others. Attempts to protect the weak were viewed as immoral because such action corrupted the struggle between individuals by shielding the weak from their natural superiors. Democracy, with its values of equity and fairness, was disdained because it was perceived to favor mediocrity and penalize excellence. Nietzsche regarded democratic values and Christian values such as humility, peace, charity, and pity as inferior to societal norms of arrogance, selfishness, and ruthlessness. In Nietzsche's world of unrestrained competition, a new race of supermen ("magnificent blond brutes") would emerge and replace the weaker races.

4. *The leadership principle*. The state is run on the principle that subordinates owe absolute obedience to immediate superiors, with everyone ultimately subordinate to the absolute leader. The absolute leaders were depicted as the personification of their respective nations. Corresponding to this principle is the belief that the leader embodies all the aspirations of the people, the leader is capable of correctly interpreting the will of the people, and the leader is infallible.

DEMOCRACY

In the purest sense, democracy can be defined as rule by or of the people. The idea of democracy was coined by the Greek historian Herodotus (ca. 485–425 B.C.). To the ancient Greeks, democracy implied rule of the people, equality under the law, popular participation in decision making, and popular control of public officials. These elements are still essential components of democracy. Two different conceptions of democracy, however, exist: direct or classical democracy and indirect or representative democracy. Classical democracy depends upon the concept of political power directly held by the people. Political philosophers such as John Locke and Jean-Jacques Rousseau supported the idea that people are essentially equal under natural law and that political power is derived from the consent of the governed. The basis of indirect democracy is that people cannot rule themselves directly but choose representatives to rule on their behalf. Political competition as well as multiple interest groups are necessary for this form of democracy to survive. Essential features of this indirect form of democracy include the following elements.[18]

1. *Voting*. The vote is probably the single most important mechanism by which citizens can express their desires. Through the vote citizens are capable of replacing their official leaders. It is assumed that elected leaders must be somewhat responsive to the wishes of the electorate in order to remain in office. Voting also helps to ensure that the interests of the minority do not prevail over the interests of the majority. It helps to ensure that all major interests in society are represented. Voting may lead to increased political awareness and can make citizens feel that the laws and decisions of the system are their own.

The right to vote, however, does not by itself guarantee that all interests in society will be equally represented. Citizen apathy, inadequate organization, and inadequate resources make it easier for those who are not disadvantaged to gain influence. John Stuart Mill stated that the ideal form of government was a government that vested authority in the entire community. Mill noted that throughout history communities that permitted self-government were superior to despotism in advancing the welfare of the community, improving the character of its citizens, and achieving the greatest happiness for the greatest number.

2. *Freedom of speech*. John Stuart Mill believed that even democracy had the tendency to limit individual liberty. Because of this tendency, Mill maintained that freedom of speech should be given absolute protection under the law. He eloquently reasoned that "if all mankind were of one opinion and only one person was of the contrary opinion, mankind would be no more justified in silencing one person, than he, if he had the power, would be justified in silencing mankind."[19] Suppressing the expression of opinion robs the human race, the existing generation, as well as posterity. Mill reasoned that if the individual opinion is right, then society is deprived of the truth; if the opinion is wrong, society loses

the clearer perception of the truth that is produced by truth's collision with error.

3. *Political equality*. The principle of political equality lies at the heart of democracy. Political equality is an essential element of democracy for the following reasons: (1) it makes it possible for all important social groups to be represented in the electoral process in proportion to their actual numbers in society; (2) political equality can increase discussion and rational voting; and (3) political equality can contribute to individual satisfaction, increasing confidence in one's environment while helping to maintain stability.

4. *Autonomy*. In reference to democratic theory, autonomy refers to the treatment of each citizen as the best judge of his or her own interests. Men and women are said to know their interests best; therefore their opinions must be treated with the utmost respect. Ordinary men and women are said to be in touch with reality and are therefore able to hold in check the potential destructive power of the intelligentsia.

5. *Majority rule*. Democratic principles require that the majority's wishes will prevail over the minority. In order to prevent a "tyranny of the majority," checks on their power are necessary. Majority rule is coupled with the principle of minority rights. Minority rights are protected by constitutional guarantees such as freedom of speech, protection of property, due process of law, and freedom of religion.

All of these specific belief sets consciously or unconsciously affect our attitudes toward public policies, our priorities, and our choice of electoral candidates. Americans are said to be less ideological than Europeans, favoring a pragmatic rather than a philosophical approach to solving problems. Americans are likely to ask questions such as "Does this idea work?" and "Are alternative ideas better?" It cannot be denied, however, that strains of the six ideologies discussed in this chapter (nationalism, communism, socialism, capitalism, fascism, and democracy) filter into our thought processes and influence our decisions. Contemporary American thought, however, should be viewed as eclectic, borrowing from major ideologies what is appealing and discarding the rest.

The discussion of the six major ideologies reviewed in this chapter is cursory and by no means intended to make readers experts in the field of political theory. This review, however, is viewed as essential for two reasons. First, a basic understanding of major thought systems will make possible a clearer understanding of contemporary American ideas. These contemporary American political thoughts are reviewed in the following chapter and include political orientations that can be identified on a "left"-to-"right" or liberal to conservative continuum. Political orientations reviewed in the following chapter include the development of traditional liberal thinking dating from the period of social activism in Great Britain, reform liberalism, or the ideas associated with populist, progressive, and socialist movements in the United States, and neoliberalism, or Democratic party attempts to develop so-called new ideas. Democratic party legislators ascribing to these new ideas include leaders such as Bruce Babbitt, Richard Gephardt, Bill Bradley, and the foremost proponent of "the politics of new ideas," Gary Hart. Traditional American conservatism--namely laissez-faire capitalism, social Darwinism, the New Right, and Neoconservatism—are also discussed in order to describe some of the ideas emanating from the right of America's political spectrum.

The beliefs reviewed in Chapter 4 did not spontaneously arise in an intellectual vacuum. It is therefore necessary to have at least a general idea of fundamental political philosophies or ideologies in order to understand how American political orientations were developed and from what broader belief system they trace their lineage.

The second reason for reviewing the six major ideologies discussed in this chapter relates to their overt or subtle influence in the development of public policies in America today. One would expect that public policies are not formulated on the basis of whim but have deeper philosophical underpinnings.

An understanding of the philosophical predispositions of policymakers would logically contribute to our understanding of the development of policy today. For example, the policy position to deregulate the airlines is related to the philosophical orientation of the Reagan administration—namely, policies promoting the "unfettered marketplace"—would be considered superior to policies promoting governmental intervention. The policy position that America needs a 600-ship navy is related to the philosophical orientation that our nation's strength, integrity, and defense are preeminent. The policy position of providing affordable health care to citizens who are beset with catastrophic illness is related to the philosophical orientation that prioritizes the need for social justice and equity. The policy position of the public sector working closely with industries in order to compete better in the international market is related to the philosophical orientation that an expansive public sector can benefit society by creating harmony between workers and managers and efficiency in general.

The foregoing review of political ideologies is somewhat elementary yet was not intended to provide insights for the discipline of political theory. The intent of the chapter was to provide a basic understanding of major political theories so that readers may better understand and evaluate contemporary currents in American political thought, which are explored in Chapter 4.

NOTES

1. Lyman T. Sargent, *Contemporary Political Ideologies* (Homewood, Ill.: The Dorsey Press, 1981), p. 16.

2. Ibid.

3. Leon Baradat, *Political Ideologies* (Englewood Cliffs, N.J.: Prentice-Hall, 1979), pp. 46–47.

4. Phillip Gove, ed., *Webster's Third New International Dictionary* (Springfield, Mass.: G & C Merriam Company, 1981).

5. Baradat, *Political Ideologies*, pp. 154–67.

6. Alfred G. Meyer, *Communism* (New York: Random House, 1984).

7. Jean-François Revel, *The Totalitarian Temptation* (New York: Doubleday, 1977).

8. William Ebenstein, *Today's ISMS* (Englewood Cliffs, N.J.: Prentice-Hall, 1964), pp. 206-12.

9. Joseph Schumpeter, *Capitalism, Socialism and Democracy* (London: George Allen & Unwin, 1981), p. 404.

10. Sidney Hook, "A New ISM for Socialism," in *Political Thought since World War II*, ed. W. J. Stankiewicz (New York: Free Press, 1964), pp. 325-30.

11. Ibid.

12. Baradat, *Political Ideologies*, p. 176.

13. Irving Kristol, *Two Cheers for Capitalism* (New York: Basic Books, 1978).

14. George Steiner and John Steiner, *Business, Government, and Society* (New York: Random House, 1985), pp. 357-58.

15. Ernest Mandel, *An Introduction to Marxist Economic Theory* (New York: Pathfinder Press, 1969).

16. Milton Friedman and Rose Friedman, *Free to Choose* (New York: Avon Books, 1979).

17. Further descriptions of fascist ideology can be found in Lyman T. Sargent, *Contemporary Political Ideologies* (Homewood, Ill.: The Dorsey Press, 1981), and Mostafa Rejai, *Comparative Political Ideologies* (New York: St. Martin's Press, 1984).

18. Dennis Thompson, *The Democratic Citizen* (London: Cambridge University Press, 1970).

19. John Stuart Mill, *On Liberty*, ed. David Spitz (New York: W. W. Norton, 1975), p. 18.

4

Contemporary American
Belief Systems

Americans must ask themselves whether there exists a distinctive American ideology. If the response to that question is affirmative, then they must inquire about the composition of that ideology. An "American ideology" conceivably includes elements of many divergent belief sets. Certainly there is a great deal of nationalism in America. Some subscribe to the view of "my country right or wrong," echoing fervent nationalist sentiment. There does not exist a viable communist or socialist party in the United States, yet many of the broad policy goals expounded by these parties are advocated by American citizens. Americans believe that equality and social justice are ideals of great value. Some Americans subscribe to programs of redistribution that will aid the poor and powerless; others believe that controls must be exerted on private industry, while others believe that the welfare state should be expanded.

The ethic of capitalism is said to be dominant in the United States. Americans subscribe to such valued concepts as the free enterprise system, individual freedom, and the absence of governmental regulations. The free exchange of services, the profit motive, competition, and the idea of private property make up the essential ingredients of our system, which has provided great material comfort for the vast majority of Americans. Along with the concept of capitalism, the ideal of democracy is also said to guide behavior in the United States. World War I, according to Woodrow Wilson, was fought not for purely nationalistic reasons but to "make the world safe for democracy." Similarly, other wars have been fought against "undemocratic" societies such as Nazi Germany in World War II, communist Korea in the 1950s, and communist Vietnam in the 1960s and 1970s. These societies were said to be totalitarian in nature, subscribing to either fascist or communist beliefs. Rights such as freedom of speech, freedom of religion, the right to assembly, the right to vote, the two-party system, and the right to bear arms are all fundamental freedoms provided in a democratic society and defended in our nation's numerous wars. These freedoms were constrained or totally absent in totalitarian societies such as those just mentioned.

Some element of almost all political thought appears to be present in the United States. Numerous individuals subscribe to "white supremacy," a doctrine that bears a likeness to the beliefs espoused by Adolf Hitler. The Ku Klux Klan is the most visible of the groups representing these thoughts. Some individuals in the United States advocate the development of more powerful business-labor-state linkages. In this scenario, groups such as business and labor would work in partnership with government to create a more efficient "corporatist" state. The creation of New York City's Emergency Financial Control Board was a model of efficient action that resulted from greater cooperation among management, labor, and government. This model is efficient; however, it resembles organizational structures developed in Italy in the late 1920s. Corporatism to many Americans too closely echoes the fascistic model of Italy and is criticized for its potential danger to democratic institutions.

The extent to which specific ideologies are relevant to contemporary political orientations in the United States is a question that must be addressed. Whether or not there exists a distinctive "American ideology" is a matter of speculation. Many analysts claim that the United States is too pragmatic to hold rigidly to a single ideology. It appears that a number of coherent belief sets may help to structure the nature of political debate in America. Some of these belief sets and their historical antecedents are described in this chapter.

AMERICAN IDEOLOGY

What is the dominant philosophy of the United States? It is believed by many analysts that the United States has a dominant philosophy reflected in the following policies: anticommunism, support of the free market, and support of constitutional government. Analysts also contend that the essential strength of the United States lies in the fact that it is essentially nonideological and its two-party system subsumes all major streams of thought. To these analysts, ideology is viewed pejoratively because it is said to be an association with the corrupting influence of "-isms" that has resulted in bloodshed and great suffering throughout the world. Americans are believed to look down on dogma and are viewed as too pragmatic to follow rigidly any specific philosophy. Perhaps Americans have always been aware of the pragmatic advice offered by Chinese leader Deng Xiaoping—that it matters not whether the color of the cat is black or white as long as it catches mice. The vitality and opportunity historically present in the United States provide fertile ground for Deng's pragmatic approach and militates against the acceptance of foreign ideologies.

In 1835, Alexis de Tocqueville published his account of the system of democracy in America. Tocqueville noted that no country paid less attention to philosophy than the United States and that Americans had no philosophical school of their own. He claimed, however, that without having taken the time to define the rules, the United States had developed a philosophy common to most of its citizens. This philosophy included the following elements: evading the bondage of class opinions, accepting tradition only as a means of information, and seeking information as a practical lesson to be used for improvement. Furthermore, Americans were said to be addicted to the practical rather than the theoretical questions of the day.[1]

Americans are not comfortable with terminology that appears to be closely linked to ideological imagery. Reo Christenson and colleagues noted that Americans see themselves as enjoying a political system called by the friendly name "democracy"—not one based on an ideology characterized by the sinister hissing sound of "-ism." He stated that Americans have an economic system commonly called "free enterprise" or at worst "a capitalistic system," but rarely "capitalism." It was observed that Americans also respond negatively to the name but not some of the programs of socialism.[2] This perspective sums up the contradictions Americans feel about ideologies and the negative labels that are associated with foreign "-isms."

In the United States, it is generally assumed that all realistic political positions fall within the parameters of liberal and conservative political orientations.[3] Because of the relevance of these philosophical perspectives to the American scene, the historical development and more recent currents emanating from these labels will be discussed in this chapter. Through this discussion of "liberalism" and "conservatism" it is hoped that a greater understanding of contemporary American belief systems will be attained. This understanding will be useful in assessing public policy issues. It is believed that if political orientations are better understood, they can begin to be controlled and more efficient public policy can then be developed.

AMERICAN LIBERALISM

Philosophical Antecedents

The contemporary American use of the term "liberalism" should not be confused with the political philosophy of "classical liberalism" developed in eighteenth-century Britain. Whereas classical liberals believed in limited government, today's liberals tend to favor using government to alleviate the problems of society. The classical liberals of Adam Smith's age are in fact philosophically much closer to the views of conservatives in America today. This is an example of the problem of time dimension discussed in Chapter 2.

The transformation of "classical liberalism" into today's conceptions of liberalism evolved over a period of time. Initially liberalism was an ideology espoused by the rising middle classes in their attacks on the privileges of the old landed aristocracy. Liberals of this period insisted on constitutional government, division of power, and clearly defined tasks for the executive, legislative, and judicial branches of government. The developing commercial interests of the day sought protection from the arbitrary acts of monarchs and other nobles and government officials through constitutional government.

Classical liberals such as John Locke and Adam Smith championed the capitalist economic system. This system, according to them, would reduce oppressive controls of the centralized state and would reward individuals for their hard work and enterprise. Under this system it was believed that any individual, regardless of social class, would be able to improve his or her living standard and quality of life. For this to be possible, it was necessary to protect these individuals from arbitrary confiscation of property by the state or aristocrats. Constitutional government, with a system of checks and balances, would decentralize power in such a way as to limit the use of arbitrary power and provide guarantees to ordinary citizens.

American liberalism can trace much of its heritage to the philosophy of utilitarianism. British authors such as Jeremy Bentham (1748–1831), James Mill (1773–1836), and John Stuart Mill (1806–73) contributed greatly to the development of this political philosophy. Bentham believed that the greatest end for society was the maximization of happiness, which was interpreted as the acquisition of the greatest happiness for the greatest number of people. According to Bentham, if every man and woman were free to maximize his or her pleasure and avoid pain, then the greatest happiness for the greatest number would result. A basic assumption of Bentham was that in a properly ordered society, the long-term interests of individuals would not be in conflict with the happiness of others. Laws would discourage antisocial behavior and more people's desire to seek pleasure in a manner conducive to the general happiness of all. This philosophy was consistent with the development of a social conscience and the use of government to address problems of society.

During the nineteenth century, liberalism became associated less with individual freedom and protection of private property and associated more with protecting the weak against abuses of power. Negative externalities associated with the Industrial Revolution, such as unemployment and poverty, were recognized and ultimately addressed by social-minded liberals in Britain such as John Stuart Mill. As a result of Mill's writings, liberalism's association with individual rights and liberties characteristic of capitalist philosophy soon was replaced by concern for justice and social equity. The government came to be perceived as the vehicle that could provide greater equity and reduce the great poverty that coexisted with the Industrial Revolution in Britain. A "new liberalism" began to develop that evolved into the current image of "liberalism."

The classical view of liberalism is rooted in the period of history called the Age of Enlightenment. This view emphasized human rationality and reasonableness. Reason was stressed rather than tradition, which was viewed as one of the precepts of the conservative philosophy. In the classical view of liberalism, written contract replaced privileged status, and individual rights replaced the rights of existing power holders.[4] Liberalism of this era (classical liberalism) supported the rights of the individual against the forces of the old Establishment. "War on Privilege" became a rallying cry of the classical liberal philosophers. These philosophers used their new rallying cry and their new political theory as weapons in their struggle against privileges of the aristocracy.

Prominent among the writers in the Age of Enlightenment was John Locke. Locke's concept of civil society was derived from two closely connected ideas: the social contract and natural law. The social contract was an agreement of the people made of their own free will. Individuals freely agreed to enter a civil or political society in order to better secure their rights.

Locke believed that people were equal only in the sense that they had the same rights under the laws of nature. The ability to defend those rights, however, was said to vary from individual to individual. It was therefore possible that injustices could result from the struggle between individuals under the laws of nature. Locke believed that in order to ensure that justice prevailed, individuals in a community should make a contract among themselves. Society would then be ruled by this social contract.

Many of Locke's ideals are embraced by both twentieth-century liberals and conservatives. Locke favored a capitalist system, believing it to be the most conducive to individual freedom and an emerging force that would weaken the status quo of his time. Locke believed, however, that property accumulation should be limited. Because of this it is surmised that he probably would have objected to the great disparities in property and wealth that began to develop in capitalist societies. These objections are predictable given that Locke maintained in his writings that no person should accumulate so much property that others would be prevented from accumulating the necessities of life.[5]

Locke assumed that the basic interests of all people in a given society were the same. This is referred to as the principle of collective interests. Locke further maintained that whatever was beneficial to the society as a whole would be beneficial to the individual. This led to the contention that the majority vote was the most essential feature of political decision making.[6] Locke's belief that the collective society was beneficial to the individual directly contrasted Adam Smith's focus on the individual as the guarantor of benefits for the whole society.

Locke's legacy to liberal thought rests in his belief that the purpose of government is to serve the people. Locke believed that government should serve the people through the state's maintenance of individual rights and liberties. This focus on government as a protector of individual rights and liberties represents Locke's legacy to American conservatives.

Jeremy Bentham was in the forefront of the second wave of liberal thinking to arise in Great Britain. Bentham advocated the use of reason to improve the lives of individuals. His basic assumption revolved around the belief that individuals seek to achieve pleasure or happiness. In Bentham's personal view, the greatest end for society would be the maximization of the greatest happiness for the greatest number. He felt that our actions and institutions should be judged by the extent to which they promote this end.[7]

Bentham did not believe that in a properly ordered society the long-term interests and happiness of individuals would be in conflict with the happiness of others in society. Laws would discourage antisocial behavior. These laws would also have the effect of molding people's desires to seek pleasure in a manner conducive to the general happiness of all.

Bentham contributed greatly to the development of the liberal ideal as we have come to know it. He did more than theorize in the abstract sense; he presented a practical standard by which to measure the value of particular policies.[8] Bentham set liberalism on a new course that could significantly improve the conditions of society. Motivation for many social reforms adopted in Great Britain between 1830 and 1850 was supplied by the writings of this political philosopher.[9]

Probably the most important political philosopher of the nineteenth century was John Stuart Mill. Like Bentham, Mill was a political activist and spent three years in the House of Commons. He supported the radical issues of his day, such as free education, trade unionism, and equal apportionment of parliamentary seats.[10] Mill believed that an active, self-helping type of person was required in a democracy. This type of individual contrasted with the passive character preferred by the government of a monarch. A focus on the desire for spontaneity, character, and originality marked Mill's writing.[11] These characteristics were said to be desirable for citizens of a democracy.

Mill argued that although democracy was the preferable form of government, even democracy could at times limit individual liberty. Because of this possibility, he believed that freedom of speech and freedom of thought should be granted absolute protection under the law.[12] This position is consistent with the First Amendment to the United States Constitution. The First Amendment, establishing the right to free speech and a free press, is perhaps the most fundamental of all freedoms in the United States. The courts in the United States have guaranteed First Amendment protections to individuals in the vast majority of cases. In 1919, Supreme Court Justice Oliver Wendell Holmes declared that free speech should be protected by the government as long as it did not represent a clear and present danger that would bring about substantive evil. Holmes's position recognizes the value of free expression in all but the most extreme circumstances, a value eloquently promoted in the nineteenth century by the writings of John Stuart Mill.

Mill's position concerning free speech and minority rights is often quoted. His fundamental position on this matter is reflected in the statement quoted previously, that mankind has no justification in suppressing the open expression of opinion because suppression of this nature would inhibit the discovery of truth.[13]

Mill was also a firm believer in the freedom of the press. He felt that in conditions of the free competition of ideas, the right ideas would prevail. This provided justification for an open, free, and uninhibited expression of minority opinions. Access of opinions through a free press would provide the type of atmosphere in which minority opinions could be expressed.

Mill is considered the first liberal philosopher to attack the laissez-faire capitalist system. His attack against the "enslaving capacity of capitalism" was so effective that few individuals categorized as liberals have supported the laissez-faire capitalist system since the time of Mill.[14] Both Bentham and Mill laid a foundation for the further development of liberal ideals. Both were interested in political activism. The liberal view that government can be used to cure some of the ills of society owes much to the lives and writings of both of these philosophers.

Legislative Antecedents

Modern social welfare legislation dates from the time of Otto von Bismark of Prussia. At a time when Marxist views were gaining popularity in Germany, Bismark urged "a little more Christian solicitude for the working man." He was fearful that class war would erupt in Germany if the state ignored the problems of the working class. In the early 1880s, motivated by those fears, Bismark introduced a comprehensive scheme of social security, offering the worker insurance against accident, sickness, and old age. Through the leadership of Bismark (the "Iron Chancellor"), the newly formed German empire became the first modern state to introduce on a fairly large scale the kind of welfare measures that are popular today.[15]

Social welfare legislation was also inaugurated in Great Britain at the turn of the twentieth century. Spurred by the writings of John Stuart Mill, policy analysts and politicians moved away from the defense of free market capitalism. Liberals began to recognize the excesses of capitalism and the need under this system to provide protections for some citizens. Liberalism's concern for greater social justice and equity produced legislation in the areas of health insurance, pensions, unemployment, and care of schoolchildren.

Sentiment for legislation gained popularity when it became recognized that the social costs of capitalism may outweigh its benefit. The Industrial Revolution in Britain had created poverty and social disruption for the majority of its people but fabulous wealth for a chosen few. In response to this inequality, people demanded that the government provide some protection for workers. This occurred at the same time as the idea of a self-regulating market providing the greatest benefit for society as a whole collapsed in the face of reality.

A "new liberalism" evolved out of "classical liberalism," which had consistently defended capitalism and individual freedom. This new liberalism addressed the issues of equity, justice, and social reform. Major concepts of this new liberalism were (1) the notion of rendering help to individuals or groups that were materially disadvantaged, (2) a desire to redesign society in such a manner as to realize ethical values among all members, (3) a desire to heighten awareness of communal ends, and (4) a desire to make people aware of the potential of the government to improve societal conditions.[16]

Advocates of social legislation believed that if industrialization and capitalism infringed upon the rights of workers to achieve a satisfactory life, then the government had a responsibility to assure the rights of workers. Old age pensions were among the first measures recommended in Britain. It was argued by proponents of old age pensions that because these benefits were payable to state servants such as soldiers, sailors, postmen, and policemen, they should also be payable to other workers. Additional benefits of old age pensions were recognized, including increasing aggregate demand, improving social justice, and creating a fuller perception of the state as the leader of a community.[17]

Old age pensions successfully expressed the sense of responsibility of the government to provide a minimum standard of living for the elderly. This provision of old age pensions is based on the recognition that individual savings are often insufficient for a comfortable life in old age and that the state has a responsibility in this area. Prominent British liberals such as L. T. Hobhouse helped to legitimize pensions through his belief that pauperism among the aged was not a result of shiftlessness, as the case may be with the younger poor, but was the normal fate of the poorer classes.

At the same time these perceptions of old age were developing, recognition was growing that unemployment was not necessarily the result of shiftlessness. Unemployment began to be viewed as a cyclical phenomenon in industrial society. Workers were periodically laid off because of slack demand. Layoffs came to be viewed as part of the capitalist system and not the fault of individual workers' laziness, irresponsibility, or character defects. This recognition in the early twentieth century led the goverment of Great Britain to accept responsibility in the area of unemployment. It was accepted that the community or the state must solve the problems foisted upon its members that did not result from individual character defects. Clearly unemployment was recognized as one of these problems.

Care of schoolchildren was another issue that attracted a good deal of attention in Britain. State care of young children was perceived as a viable means of breaking the cycle of social distress that was said to be characteristic of the lower classes in Britain in the early 1900s. Liberal publications such as *The Speaker* and *The Nation* claimed that it was the duty of the state to insist that every child in elementary school have the physical sustenance required for development. It was believed that parents should provide the necessary level of sustenance, but in the event of their refusal or inability, it should be supplied by voluntary means or by the local government.[18]

A number of motives accompanied the sentiment to provide food for school-age children. Children were viewed as a natural resource indispensable to the well-being of the community as a whole. Their development, therefore, was regarded as too important to be left entirely to individual parents. This sentiment, combined with humanitarian motives, put pressure on the government for legislation to deal with the care of schoolchildren.

Health care is still another area in which the government of Britain accepted responsibility for the provision of services. The Insurance Act of 1911 provided national health and unemployment insurance for all workers. Joint responsibility was assumed by workers and the state in order to ensure this protection. The British system of health care or "socialized medicine" is referred to by many in the United States as a poor health system, yet it is considered superior to American health care from the perspective of cost. The United States has adopted some of Britain's features of health care with Medicaid for the poor and Medicare for the aged. The United States has not gone as far as Britain, however, in providing free health care for all citizens of the nation. In other areas, such as old age pensions, unemployment insurance, and the care of schoolchildren, the United States has accepted government responsibilities similar to the British initiatives.

AMERICAN REFORM LIBERALISM

Kenneth Hoover stated that reform liberalism brought together ideas taken from populism, progressivism, and even socialism. These ideas are said to have come together in Franklin Delano Roosevelt's New Deal and reached a peak in Lyndon Johnson's Great Society. Recently, the values of reform liberalism appear to have declined in influence as a result of an assault by conservative elements in the nation.[19] Reform liberals are noted by their desire to use governmental power to remedy the inequalities of the marketplace. Early reformers sought to gain greater control over the marketplace for the "little people" of the United States, represented by farmers and laborers. Farmers of the Midwest were among the first groups to organize against the interests of big business, spearheading the movement for state regulation of the railroad industry.

Between 1870 and 1874, four midwestern states, responding to strong pressure from farmers, passed what have become known as the Granger laws. These laws regulated the prices railroads, warehouses, and grain elevators could charge. Originally, the Supreme Court upheld the constitutionality of these laws, which regulated business and limited their ability to charge prices as they saw fit.[20] Following the original upholding of the Granger laws in 1877, the views of the Court changed noticeably to favor the interests of business. In 1886, the Supreme Court reversed itself, holding state regulation of interstate commerce to be unconstitutional.[21]

The will of the people would not be blocked by the ruling of the Court. Legislative action was sought in Congress, and in 1887 the first modern regulatory agency, the Interstate Commerce Commission (ICC) was created by the Interstate Commerce Act. This act prohibited unfair pricing practices and required railroads to make rates public as well as report them to the five-person Commerce Commission. The Act required that railroad rates be "reasonable and just"; the courts eventually defined the wording more precisely. The passage of the Interstate Commerce Act in 1887 represented a great victory in the battle between the "little people" (in this case, small farmers) and corporate giants represented by the railroad industry.

The populism that spawned the ICC sought a system in which power would be more justly distributed. To reach this goal, cooperation rather than confrontation with those in power was pursued. Alan Grimes stated that one of the specific objectives of the National Grange was "to foster mutual understanding and cooperation." The Grange basically sought cheaper methods of transporting crops to the market and eliminating the middleman in farm marketing. It expressly disavowed any assumptions of inevitable conflict or antagonisms that were commonly associated with more radical thought.[22]

The Populist party attained some degree of power in the late nineteenth century. John Diggins claimed that in the 1890s the Populist party could control or influence a dozen state legislatures, four senators, and over fifty congressmen.[23] The Populist party did not endure long, however, and declined after 1896 largely because much of its program was accepted by progressive Republicans and Democrats. The two-party system was able to coopt new ideas under old party banners, as they have often done in the past.

The view that the United States was not realizing the democratic ideals that had been established with the writing of the Constitution represented a fundamental position of the Progressive movement. In an effort to curb the power of the strong and protect the weak from oppression, Progressives were able to enact a good deal of economic and political reforms. Economic reforms of the Progressive era included the strengthening of railroad regulation, the eventual passage of the progressive income tax, the more vigorous enforcement of the Sherman Anti-Trust Act, the strengthening of child labor laws, and municipal ownership of public utilities. Political reforms included direct primaries, direct election of representatives to the United States Senate, direct legislation, the referendum, recall, and the secret ballot.[24]

Intellectual leaders of the Progressive movement included Herbert Croly (1869–1924), Walter Weyl (1873–1919), and

Woodrow Wilson (1856–1924). Croly called for a new Hamil-
tónian program of greater government action in order to control the powerful and assist the weak. He believed that local
and sectional special interest groups could be absorbed into a
national moral pattern, which would turn groups away from
seeking private advantage and lead them toward pursuit of
the public good. In his classic work *The Promise of American
Life*, Croly decried monied interests and called for regulation
of the "few irresponsible men" who needed monitoring.
Croly believed that the freedom our tradition grants to individuals was beneficial only up to a certain point. He stated
that because of excesses of "money people," the "peculiar
freedom which the American tradition and organization have
granted to the individual" was not merely harmful but could
be fatal if not controlled. Croly called for regulation of the
"chaotic individualism" that is a feature of our society:

Effective regulation there must be; and it must be regulation which will
strike, not at the symptoms of the evil, but at its roots. The existing
concentration of wealth and financial power in the hands of a few irresponsible men is the inevitable outcome of the chaotic individualism of
our political and economic organization, while at the same time it is
inimical to democracy, because it tends to erect political abuses and
social inequalities into the system.[25]

The high-water mark of the Progressive movement was the
election of Woodrow Wilson as president in 1912. Wilson
sought to increase popular freedom by controlling economic
interests in the nation. He attempted to use the powers of the
national government to revitalize the dignity, individuality,
and freedom of the average person. He believed that (1) in
our society political power had gravitated into the hands of
those possessing economic power; (2) economic power did
not by itself constitute fitness for political control; (3) increased economic subservience to the minority was sapping
the strength of personal and responsible individualism; and
(4) popular freedom was held at bay when the most vital

decisions were made by economic elites who were beyond the reach of popular control.[26]

While Wilson's brand of progressivity gained a wider following and greater electoral success, a more radical interpretation of American society also began to attract followers in the late nineteenth and early twentieth centuries. This radical interpretation of American society is associated with the Socialist party and the ideology of socialism. Daniel DeLeon (1852–1914) and Eugene Debs (1855–1926) are two of the better-known individuals associated with American socialism. DeLeon was unable to broaden the appeal of the Socialist Labor party because of his strict adherence to orthodox Marxism. Debs, on the other hand, was more flexible and attracted an assortment of reformers. He maintained that class conflict could be solved peacefully by compromise and adjustment. In his 1912 acceptance speech as the presidential candidate of the Socialist party, Debs stated that the mission of the Socialist party was to establish industrial and social democracy. He urged workers to steadily organize for the day when they would take control of industry and make the right to work "as inviolate as the right to breathe the breath of life."[27]

American reform liberalism is still considered a force in American politics, although its ability to influence policy seems to have declined in recent years. In a contemporary context, reform liberalism is characterized by intense concern for social problems such as poverty, unemployment, war, racism, and deterioration of the environment. This concern is coupled with the conviction that the capitalist ideology of the United States cannot or will not cope with the pressing problems of society.[28]

Reform liberalism as well as liberalism in general, with its emphasis on equality and social justice, is viewed critically by many today. Many contemporary politicians wish to distance themselves from policies that are perceived as "failures of liberalism." These politicians are for the most part former liberals who today prefer to call themselves neoliberals. The agenda of these neoliberals is qualitatively different from that of reform liberals and liberals of the Roosevelt-Johnson eras.

NEOLIBERALISM

It should be no secret by now that the popularity of the liberal philosophy has declined since Franklin Roosevelt's New Deal and Lyndon Johnson's Great Society. Liberal candidates such as Hubert Humphrey in 1968, George McGovern in 1972, and Walter Mondale in 1984 all were defeated in presidential elections. McGovern and Mondale, running against much more conservative opponents, were defeated by huge margins. In senatorial races, well-known liberals such as Birch Bayh of Indiana, Frank Church of Idaho, John Culver of Iowa, and George McGovern of South Dakota all were defeated in 1980. Liberals were said to be too closely associated with narrow special interest groups. An association of liberals with groups such as organized labor, gays, pacifists, women's liberationists, blacks, and other minorities were believed to cost liberals support with mainstream Americans who were said to represent a "silent majority."

In response to the declining popularity of liberal views, a new group of politicians termed "neoliberals" have gained popularity. Neoliberals claim that they retain allegiance to liberal ideals such as justice, fair play, and compassion; however, they want to free themselves from discredited social programs of the liberal era. They recognize the need for more government-business cooperation in order to reverse the decline in the United States's manufacturing sector. Other features of the neoliberal agenda include compulsory national service, centralized economic planning, high-tech industrialization, and a strong national defense.[29] The neoliberal ideology is said to be represented by politicians such as Gary Hart of Colorado, Bill Bradley of New Jersey, Albert Gore of Tennessee, Bruce Babbitt of Arizona, Richard Gephardt of Missouri, and Leon Panetta of California. Contemporary Democrats such as these leaders are said to be retreating from the old ideals of liberalism and are ready to accept something new.

Linda Medcalf and Kenneth Dolbeare stated that three primary principles exist for neoliberals: (1) recognition of the absolute necessity of economic growth; (2) recognition that in our changing world economy, government policies are crucial to private sector success; and (3) belief that the Soviet Union remains a hostile and expansionist nation that has now built up its military power to a dangerous level. Within the context of these three overriding principles, neoliberalism advocates a humane society with women and minorities afforded full citizenship rights.[30]

In general, a dominant theme of neoliberalism is the rejection of self-interest as a basis for action. Charles Peters, in his "Neoliberal's Manifesto," stated that the politics of selfishness accompanied with an adversarial approach to problems has been disastrous for the nation. He advocated instead "a rebirth of patriotism, a rebirth of devotion to the interests of the national community, of the convictions that we're all in this together and that therefore fair play and justice for everyone is the vital concern for us all."[31]

Other themes of neoliberalism include (1) freeing entrepreneurs for risk-taking to create new and better products, (2) returning the concept of equality from equality of outcomes to the older conception of equality of opportunity, (3) concern for the public school system, and (4) a more pessimistic view of human nature than that of reform liberals.[32]

Neoliberals have broken with what they perceived to be unworkable concepts. In terms of their beliefs on foreign policy issues and issues of economic growth, they are in closer agreement with American conservatives than with their former brethren, the New Deal liberals. It is necessary to review the philosophical development of American conservatism to understand this schism more clearly.

AMERICAN CONSERVATISM

Conservatism, like liberalism, has numerous interpretations. Classic conservatism exemplified by the writing of Edmund Burke (1729–97) emphasized the importance of tradition and continuity. According to Burke, society represents the accumulation of experience and wisdom. Principles and rules of behavior that have evolved over time therefore should be conserved. This would have the advantage of holding the destructive tendencies of individuals in check. Burke also believed that the use of government will not necessarily help to improve the human condition, and that if people come to rely on the government, they will eventually lose their ability to take care of themselves.

Another dominant feature of conservatism is its emphasis on individualism and freedom. Government is viewed with suspicion by conservatives because it is seen as inhibiting innovation and economic growth. According to Milton Friedman, whenever there exist large elements of individual freedom, some measure of material progress occurs for ordinary citizens, but wherever the state undertakes to control economic activity in detail, ordinary citizens have a low standard of living and little control over their own destiny. The following characteristics are generally accepted to represent conservative political thought: (1) resistance to change, (2) reverence for tradition, (3) distrust of human reason, (4) rejection of the use of government to improve the human condition, and (5) anti-egalitarianism.[33] Elements of these characteristics can be found in American political discourse today. These elements are also found in the statements of the neoconservative movement and the New Right.

Historical Development

Dominant themes of American conservatism include the acceptance of inequality in society, the acceptance of a laissez-faire economy, and the promotion of a minimalist government. At the turn of the century American conservative thought also reflected the philosophy of social Darwinism espoused by authors such as Herbert Spencer and William Sumner, and industrialists such as Andrew Carnegie.

Theories of competition discussed by Carnegie were refined in the writings of Herbert Spencer. Spencer applied Darwin's biological theory of evolution to the social development of man. Spencer believed that nature's process of winnowing out the weak and shiftless was necessary and governed the development of the human race. Life, according to Spencer, was a ruthless struggle for survival. As each generation eliminated the unfit, the "breed" was believed to improve. Social legislation was unnatural, according to Spencer, because it impeded nature's method of improving the species. Carnegie focused on the belief that competition was essential for progress to evolve. Carnegie contended that competition was "best for the race because it insures the survival of the fittest in every department." He accepted concentration of power and wealth as being "not only beneficial but essential for the future progress of the race."[34]

The philosophy of social Darwinism was also advanced by William Sumner (1840–1910). Sumner vigorously attacked socialism's efforts to ameliorate the hardships of life. He exalted the principle of liberty and the system of nature that rewarded some and punished others. Sumner claimed that adopting socialism's principles would go against the laws of nature by favoring the survival of the unfittest.

If we do not like it [the system of nature], and we try to amend it, there is only one way in which we can do it. We can take from the better and give it to the worse. We can deflect the penalties of those who have done ill and throw them on those who have done better. We can take the rewards from those who have done better and give them to those who have done worse. We shall thus lessen the inequalities. We shall favor the survival of the unfittest, and we shall accomplish this by destroying liberty.[35]

Individualism, social Darwinism, and laissez-faire economics remain features of conservative thought in the United States today. More recent developments in conservative philosophy such as the rise of the "New Right" and of the "neoconservatives" have thrust the conservative movement into a more prominent position than was the case in the recent past. These contemporary conservative movements are described below.

THE NEW RIGHT

Emphasis on moral values is a dominant feature of the New Christian Right and the larger group from which it derives, the New Right. Moralist themes helped to elect Jimmy Carter president in 1976 and Ronald Reagan in 1980 and 1984. The New Christian Right blames the decline of the United States on a decline in the moral character of the nation. It is believed that in order to return the United States to a position of greatness, values such as work, family, and neighborhood must be prioritized. According to this perspective, Americans must reject "secular humanism" and return to the laws of God. Only then will the United States become a great nation again.

The New Christian Right claims credit for nominating Ronald Reagan in 1980 instead of hopefuls such as John Connelly (who enjoyed the support of big business), Robert Dole, George Bush, and Howard Baker. They also claim credit for the election of 25 out of 30 seats in the House of Representatives, targeted in 1980. The New Christian Right also has gained a great deal of confidence in its ability to win elections. Pat Robertson reflected this view with the sentiment that Americans were now able to defeat liberals who fail to "control dope, pornography, abortion, feminism, and moral decay."[36]

The New Right is significantly distinct from what has come to be known as the Old Right. Paul Weyrich explained that the Old Right was strongly intellectual, pursuing a level of discourse above the language of ordinary people. The New Right, in contrast, is said to reach the common people through a direct discussion of "gut" social issues such as crime, abortion, busing, and the spread of pornography. The Old Right emphasized the primacy of laissez-faire economic principles, whereas the New Right realizes that people have come to expect certain things of government and that it is possible to extend public services without destroying the free enterprise system.[37]

The New Right is pragmatic in its attempt to mobilize middle-class dissent. As previously stated, it eschews highbrow philosophical discourse and addresses gut-level issues. Richard Viguerie, a political strategist of the New Right, contends that conservatives can build a majority coalition in the United States by emphasizing social issues such as abortion, the role of gays in society, pornography, gun control, street crime, busing, drug abuse, capital punishment, and the ERA. It is believed by advocates of the New Right that their positions on these issues can attract large numbers of "social conservatives" that traditionally have been aligned with the Democratic party. The New Right views the United States as on the decline and in need of community work, and political activity by church activists.[38] The New Right supported the candidacy of Ronald Reagan, and many credit it for his election. The presidential bid of Pat Robertson is another indication that the New Right may be a viable force on the American political scene for many years to come.

The New Right supposedly benefits from society's rejection of liberal ideology and social engineering. Social engineering is defined as a massive manipulation of a society's structure and values aimed at bringing about desired social change in the direction considered best by a small elite. The New Right also benefits from purported bureaucratic and judicial tyranny in the face of popular opposition. Racial quotas are an example of this so-called judicial tyranny and are perceived

to be part of the liberal program that has driven social conservatives out of the Democratic party. The dissatisfied Democrats are welcomed by the New Right and said to make up
an important element of the group. The social conservatives
who are departing from the Democratic party fold are largely
white Southerners and blue-collar Northerners who previously
voted for Franklin Roosevelt, Harry Truman, and John
Kennedy.

The New Right differs from other conservative groups in
history. Samuel Francis stated that the New Right was unlike
almost any other conservative group in history because it was
excluded from the centers of real power. Because the New
Right is considered to be excluded from the centers of power
in the country, it finds a radical anti-establishment approach
to politics better suited to achieve its goals. The Christian
ministry, working-class individuals, and former liberals who
have lost enthusiasm for liberal causes make up significant
proportions of this evolving conservative group.[39] This movement, as well as the neoconservative movement, has breathed
fresh life into American conservative thought.

NEOCONSERVATISM

Neoconservatism is articulated by former liberals such as
Irving Kristol, Daniel Bell, and Daniel Patrick Moynihan.
Unlike traditional conservatives, neoconservatives accept the
essentials of the welfare state and recognize the hazards of an
unregulated free market economy. Neoconservatives accept
the welfare state only to a limited extent and are said to be
opposed to a "paternalistic" state.

Neoconservatives are respectful of traditional values and
institutions such as religion and the family. They affirm
notions of equality of opportunity but reject the idea of
equal distribution and are highly critical of post-Vietnam iso-
lationism. Peter Steinfels summed up the major streams of
neoconservative thought. First, neoconservatives are said to

believe that a crisis of authority has overtaken the United States and the Western world in general. Governing institutions are perceived to have lost their legitimacy, and the confidence of leading elites is perceived to be sapped. As a result of these problems, social stability and the legacy of liberal civilization are said to be threatened.[40]

A second point developed in neoconservative thought is that the current crisis in the United States is primarily a cultural crisis, a matter of values, and morals. Although this crisis has causes and consequences on the level of socioeconomic structures, neoconservatives, unlike the Left, tend to think that these structures perform well. The problem is viewed as that of convictions gone slack and morals gone loose, not as a problem with the system itself. A third fundamental belief of the neoconservative movement is that government is said to be the victim of "societal overload." By attempting to do too much, government has naturally failed and thereby undermined its own authority.[41]

Neoconservatism contains a distinct element of nay-saying and pessimism. Medcalf and Dolbeare stated that neoconservatives are heir to the cautious side of liberalism and the first major "fragment" to detach itself from post-1960s liberalism.[42] Midge Decter characterized neoconservatism as "a bitter disillusionment with socialism and hyperactive liberalism with a high degree of American patriotism."[43] Neoconservatives are also recognized for their objection to the "new class" of social engineers who are employed in efforts to change the behavior of individuals. Among other elements of neoconservatism, radical demands of the left in the United States during the 1960s are believed to represent an excess of democracy. Neoconservatives also believe that government is trying to do too much in the area of social policy. As a result of these efforts, government is said to be "overloaded."

Neoconservatives are commonly associated with intellectuals without a popular following. This is in contrast to the New Right, where grass-roots support is actively courted.

Whereas the neoconservative movement can be viewed as intellectual and therefore somewhat elitist, evidence exists that distrust of liberal policies of the 1960s is widespread throughout the general population. Electoral behavior of the post-Johnson period indicates that the liberal philosophy has declined as a force in American politics.

DECLINE OF LIBERALISM'S SALIENCE

Erosion of support for liberal causes provides one possible explanation of contemporary public policy developments. The perception that an ever-expanding public sector is desirable has been vigorously attacked in recent years. Theodore H. White stated that the election of 1980 marked the rejection of a whole system of ideas that dominated American life since the early 1960s. He maintained that the Great Society was an example of good will being pushed too far and being ultimately rejected by the voters.[44] George Will noted that the Democratic party (with its association with liberal policies) has not received a majority of the white vote since the Johnson landslide of 1964.[45] The detachment of "neoliberals" from discredited social programs of the 1960s also indicates that politicians in the Democratic party are aware of voter dissatisfaction with liberalism. Theodore Lowi recognized the extent of this dissatisfaction, claiming that the sixties resulted in a "spectacular paradox" whereby the expansion of the welfare state was accompanied by a growing sense of distrust toward public figures.[46]

In the late 1960s, a group of prominent social scientists including Daniel Bell, Nathan Glazer, Seymour Martin Lipset, Irving Kristol, and James Q. Wilson banded together to analyze failures of liberal policies. This group united to make a stand against what they called the "armies of alienation" that were associated with liberal sentiment.[47] The perspective of this group is also enunciated by Norman Podhoretz in his publication *Commentary*. Podhoretz claimed that because many of the contributors to *Commentary* had some experience with the counterculture movement, they could not be easily discredited by liberals and would not be intimidated.[48]

Podhoretz claimed that the principle of equality of results enunciated in the 1960s represented an assault on what was perhaps the single most distinctive feature of the American tradition: the idea that social justice is satisfied by the distribution of rewards on the basis of individual merit. Podhoretz maintained that it was unrealistic to demand that the ultimate goal of society be the equal distribution of rewards to all. Podhoretz denounced the fact that "under the new egalitarian banner, and in the name of justice, it was possible to denigrate the pursuit of success as well as the values traditionally associated with it (ambition, discipline, and work)."[49]

Irving Kristol, another critic of liberalism, maintained that a problem of the liberal ideology was that it created a welfare state that was on a collision course with working-class psychology.[50] Celeste MacLeod recognized this dilemma, noting that problems with liberal philosophies became evident when growing numbers of the working class turned against big government, political idealists, and the entire spectrum of the counterculture, rather than against groups (that Marxist ideology would expect) such as multinational banks and multinational corporations. MacLeod stated that contrary to Marxist expectations, blue-collar workers lined up against idealists and counterculturists from the "affluent society." In the 1960s, archenemies of workers were said to be "hippies" and antiwar activists; in the 1970s, the new enemies were environmentalists. In the mid-1970s, workers shocked environmentalists by opposing what they called "college-educated optionnaires" from the affluent society who believed that the survival of obscure animals was more important than jobs.[51]

Ken Auletta and Robert Eisner attacked liberalism in promoting the theory that liberal philosophies had been captured by greedy special interest groups. These groups were said to be more interested in profiting from the growth of the

welfare state than in working toward concrete goals. Physi-
cians, attorneys, administrators, realtors, and construction
companies were some of the groups that had vested interests
in the expansion of programs that assisted the poor.[52] Many
liberal programs were viewed as "leaky sieves" in that money
would never reach the poor but would leak away to administrators and others who could milk the system.

Conservatives such as Milton Friedman claimed that liberalism declined in popularity because of its inability to allocate
resources efficiently. To Friedman, the individual spending
his or her own money in a competitive free market would
provide the best means of ensuring efficiency. Liberal programs, however, involved bureaucratic decision making
whereby someone (administrator) spent someone else's
money (taxpayers') on someone else (recipient of the program). This would, according to Friedman, almost guarantee
inefficiency because administrators would have little incentive to economize or receive the greatest value. Friedman
believed that when "human kindness" of bureaucrats rather
than the "much stronger and more dependable spur of self-
interest" was involved, there would be no guarantee that
money would be spent efficiently. There was almost a guarantee that the money would be spent inefficiently. He stated
that not only would inefficiency result but that this practice
would lead to a situation of one group possessing a feeling of
"God-like power" while the other group would be left with a
feeling of "childlike dependence."[53]

This chapter has reviewed contemporary political thought
as well as the historical antecedents of that thought. It is
hoped that this discussion will provide insight into how fundamental value systems in the United States may affect our
thinking and influence public policy. Part II empirically
explores linkages between political philosophy and budget
policy. Given that thoughts guide action, it is reasonable to
assume that political orientations influence public sector

priorities and methods of achieving goals. The influence of political perspective on budget outputs is evident because these orientations shape attitudes toward important policy decisions such as level of spending, expenditure priorities, methods of taxing, and methods of stimulating economic growth. The issue of "political" versus "rational" means of formulating budget policy is also discussed in Part II.

NOTES

1. Alexis de Tocqueville, *Democracy in America* (New York: New American Library, 1956).

2. Reo Christenson, Dan Jacobs, Mostafa Rejai, and Herbert Waltzer, *Ideologies and Modern Politics* (London: Thomas Nelson & Sons, 1971), p. 5.

3. Richard T. Saeger, *American Government and Politics A Neoconservative Approach* (Glenview, Ill.: Scott, Foresman, 1982), p. 23.

4. E. K. Bramsted and K. J. Melhuish, eds., *Western Liberalism* (London: The Chaucer Press, 1978), p. xvii.

5. Leon Baradat, *Political Ideologies* (Englewood Cliffs, N.J.: Prentice-Hall, 1979), p. 61.

6. Ibid., p. 62.

7. Bramsted and Melhuish, *Western Liberalism*, p. 20.

8. Baradat, *Political Ideologies*, p. 94.

9. Ibid.

10. Ibid., p. 96.

11. Bramsted and Melhuish, *Western Liberalism*, p. 249.

12. Baradat, *Political Ideologies*, p. 97.

13. Bramsted and Melhuish, *Western Liberalism*, p. 79.

14. Baradat, *Political Ideologies*, p. 97.

15. Milton Friedman and Rose Friedman, *Free to Choose* (New York: Avon Books, 1979), p. 88.

16. Michael Freeden, *The New Liberalism: An Ideology of Social Reform* (Oxford: Oxford University Press, 1978), p. 20.

17. "Pensions and the Poor Law," *Nation*, quoted in Freeden, *The New Liberalism*, p. 203.

18. Freeden, *The New Liberalism*, p. 222.

19. Kenneth Hoover, *Ideology and Political Life* (Monterey, Calif.: Brooks/Cole, 1986), p. 62.

20. *Munn v. Illinois*, 94 U.S. 113 (1876).

21. *Cincinnati, New Orleans and Texas Pacific Railway Co. v. I.C.C.*, 162 U.S. 184 (1896).

22. Alan Grimes, *American Political Thought* (New York: Holt, Rinehart and Winston, 1960), p. 357.

23. John Diggins, *The American Left in the Twentieth Century* (New York: Harcourt Brace Jovanovich, 1973), p. 41.

24. Grimes, *American Political Thought*, p. 387.

25. Quoted in Michael B. Levy, *Political Thought in America* (Homewood, Ill.: The Dorsey Press, 1982), p. 328.

26. Grimes, *American Politcal Thought*, p. 393.

27. Levy, *Political Thought in America*, p. 308.

28. Kenneth Dolbeare and Patricia Dolbeare, *American Ideologies* (Chicago: Rand McNally, 1978), p. 73.

29. Randall Rothenberg, "The Neoliberal Club," *Esquire*, February 1982, p. 38.

30. Linda Medcalf and Kenneth Dolbeare, *Neopolitics American Political Ideas in the 1980s* (Philadelphia: Temple University Press, 1985), p. 56.

31. Charles Peters, "A Neoliberal's Manifesto," *The Washington Monthly*, May 1983, pp. 9-18.

32. Medcalf and Dolbeare, *Neopolitics*, p. 62.

33. Lyman T. Sargeant, *Contemporary Political Ideologies* (Homewood, Ill.: The Dorsey Press, 1981), p. 96.

34. Andrew Carnegie, "Wealth," *North American Review* (June 1889), cited in Levy, *Political Though in America*, p. 268.

35. Quoted in Grimes, *American Political Thought*, p. 306.

36. Erling Jorstad, *The Politics of Moralism* (Minneapolis: Augsbert Publishing House, 1981).

37. Paul Weyrich, "Blue Collar or Blue Blood: The New Right Compared to the Old Right," in *The New Right Papers*, ed. Robert Whitaker (New York: St. Martin's Press, 1982).

38. Richard Viguerie, "Ends and Means," in Whitaker, *The New Right Papers*, pp. 26-35.

39. Samuel T. Francis, "Message from MARS: The Social Politics of the New Right," in Whitaker, *The New Right Papers*, pp. 64-83.

40. Peter Steinfels, *The Neoconservatives The Men Who Are Changing America's Politics* (New York: Simon and Schuster, 1980).

41. Ibid.

42. Medcalf and Dolbeare, *Neopolitics*, p. 130.

43. Quoted in *The Weekly* (Seattle), 16 November 1983.

44. "America's Problem: Trying to Do Everything for Everybody," *U.S. News and World Report*, 5 July 1982, p. 59.

45. Robert Hoy, "Lid on a Boiling Pot," in Whitaker, *The New Right Papers*, p. 101.

46. Theodore Lowi, *The End of Liberalism* (New York: W. W. Norton, 1969), p. 50.

47. Norman Podhoretz, *Breaking Ranks* (New York: Harper & Row, 1979), p. 305.

48. Ibid., p. 307.

49. Ibid., p. 292.

50. Irving Kristol, *Two Cheers for Capitalism* (New York: Basic Books, 1978), p. 213.

51. Celeste MacLeod, *Horatio Alger, Farewell: The End of the American Dream* (New York: Seaview Books, 1980), p. 178.

52. Michael Harrington, "Why the Welfare State Breaks Down," in *Beyond the Welfare State*, ed. Irving Howe (New York: Schocken Books, 1982), pp. 16-41.

53. Friedman and Friedman, *Free to Choose*, p. 108.

Part II

IDEOLOGIES AND BUDGET POLICY

5

Ideological Influences on Budget Outputs

This chapter empirically explores linkages between political orientation and public policy outputs. It is believed that public policy budget outputs will be found to correspond with the ideological predispositions of a given community. In this chapter governmental units will be identified along a liberal-conservative continuum and their association with predicted policy outputs based on ideology will be assessed. In terms of budget outputs, it is predicted that jurisdictions characterized as conservative elect public officials who desire (1) low aggregate levels of total public spending, (2) balanced budgets, (3) spending on "essential" rather than social programs, and (4) more regressive means of taxation. It is assumed that jurisdictions characterized as liberal elect public officials whose views differ. These representatives predictably would hold the following predispositions: (1) desire for a more expansive public sector and therefore a desire for relatively high levels of total spending; (2) a desire to borrow, if possible, to meet the demands society places upon government; (3) a desire for relatively high levels of spending on social programs to meet the needs of the poor; and (4) a desire for a more progressive means of taxation.

The extent to which jurisdictions follow an ideologically predicted pattern of outputs is an empirical question that can be determined from an examination of the historical data. The association between ideology and budget outputs will be explored in this chapter on the international, national, state, and local levels to determine the linkage between ideologies of jurisdictions and the public policy outputs characteristic of those jurisdictions. It is believed that the data will provide evidence for the assertion that budget outputs are related to ideological predispositions of given polities.

IDEOLOGY AND BUDGETS

International Level

Ideology contributes to our perceptions of the world by providing a philosophy by which to judge events. The importance of values or philosophy in the budgetary process has long been recognized. V. O. Key, Jr., stated that the fundamental dilemma of budgeting revolved around the issue of choice between divergent value preferences lacking a common denominator. Therefore, according to Key, questions of how to most advantageously utilize public resources became issues of political philosophy and value preference.[1]

Key was not alone in recognizing the role values play in determining budget outputs. William Gorham, head of the Urban Institute, reiterated Key's position, stating that the "grand decisions" such as how much health, how much welfare, and which groups in the population shall benefit were really questions of value judgment.[2] These value judgments were in turn greatly influenced by the broader philosophical frameworks that we commonly call ideologies.

In the United States, philosophical differences exist within the parameters of generally accepted rules. There is general consensus concerning the desirability of certain protections such as the right to free speech, open elections, a "safety net" provided by the government, and freedom of religion. Within these broadly accepted parameters, differences of opinion exist. In the United States, differences in philosophy of government are identified along a liberal-conservative continuum.

Groups such as the Americans for Democratic Action (ADA) and the Committee on Political Education (COPE) engage in rating legislators on the basis of their voting records. These groups numerically score congressional representatives based on their votes on carefully selected bills. High ADA scores relate to a large number of "correct" votes, the "correct" vote being defined as a positive vote for a liberal issue. Low scores relate to a high number of "incorrect" votes, the "incorrect" vote being interpreted as a vote that did not correspond with the liberal position. Representatives that are assigned high ADA scores are viewed as liberal, whereas representatives with low scores are viewed as conservative. These scores can then be used to characterize representatives from all over the nation.

Major philosophical differences exist within the United States. In 1982, the Americans for Democratic Action assigned scores of zero to Senator Jesse Helms and Senator John East of North Carolina while Senator Howard Metzenbaum of Ohio received an ADA score of 100.[3] These scores represent ideological extremes that exist within the United States Congress.

Ideological differences also exist on the international level. There are great differences in philosophy between the Marxist, "Eastern bloc" nations and the capitalist, "Western bloc" nations. Within these blocs less extreme ideological differences can also be found. In regard to the communist nations, Albania is said to be more of a closed society than East Germany. Similarly, in the Western bloc nations, the philosophy of the United States is said to differ from philosophies espoused in other nations. The United States is said to inculcate more of a probusiness and procapitalist orientation than nations of Western Europe.[4] Whether or not these stated differences in philosophical orientation translate into specific policy differences is a question that will be investigated later in this chapter. Budgetary data from the United States and Western Europe indicate that disparities in both tax and expenditure policies do in fact exist. These differences are in the direction one would expect based on an understanding of political ideology.

Despite the common complaint heard in the United States about a social security program that is out of hand, the level of social security spending in the United States as a proportion of gross national product (GNP) is significantly lower than in Western Europe. Social security spending in the United States for the period 1975–77 was 13.6 percent of GNP compared to 28.0 percent in Sweden, 27.1 percent in the Netherlands, 24.8 percent in France, 24.4 percent in Denmark, 23.7 percent in West Germany, and 17.2 percent in the United Kingdom.

Differences were also found between the United States and Western Europe in regard to taxes. Corresponding with ideological differences, American tax collections as a percentage of GNP in 1980 were significantly lower than corresponding tax levels in Western Europe. In the United States, tax collections as a percentage of GNP were 30.7 percent compared to Western European tax collections, ranging from Sweden's 49.9 percent to 35.9 percent collected in the United Kingdom.[5]

High individual tax rates in Western Europe have led to efforts to avoid payment. Specifically, high tax rates in Sweden and West Germany are cited as major factors contributing to the change in residency of popular celebrities such as tennis stars Bjorn Borg and Boris Becker, who choose to declare official residency in the lightly taxed municipality of Monaco. It is reasonable to assume that tax policies of their native countries had something to do with their decisions.

In general, the philosophical foundations of the United

States appear to be much more conservative than the corresponding political philosophies found in Western Europe. The acceptance of conservative philosophies in the United States is, however, by no means monolithic and varies over time. Certain periods of American history can be characterized as more liberal or conservative. For example, the administrations of Presidents Franklin Roosevelt and Lyndon Johnson are considered much more liberal than the administrations of Presidents Herbert Hoover and Ronald Reagan. These ebbs and flows of liberal and conservative philosophies in the United States, as well as their association with public policy outputs, are explored later.

National Level

The tradition of classical liberalism, with its respect for private property and individual rights, has always been strong in the United States.[6] This tradition has been strong, perhaps even dominant, in the United States yet has not been accepted in all periods of the nation's history. Attitudes of Populists, Progressives, and New Deal liberals have also helped to shape American policy. To varying degrees, certain periods and certain administrations were influenced by these philosophies. In other periods conservative philosophies were more dominant.

Progressive and liberal views are said to have influenced the administrations of Theodore Roosevelt, Woodrow Wilson, Franklin D. Roosevelt, John Kennedy, and Lyndon Johnson. Conservative views are associated with the administrations of American presidents such as Calvin Coolidge, Herbert Hoover, and Ronald Reagan. Other administrations such as those of Jimmy Carter, Richard Nixon, Gerald Ford, and Dwight D. Eisenhower appear to fall somewhere in the middle of the ideology continuum.

Given the rough characterization of these administrations, policy differences by ideology are identified. Size of aggregate national budgets for the period 1921 to 1984 are investigated

IDEOLOGICAL BUDGETING

Table 1
Budget Outlays as a Percentage of GNP, 1921-84

Years	% of GNP	Period
1921-1933	4.9	Republican Conservatism
1934-1941	9.8	New Deal Influences
1942-1946	35.7	World War II Mobilization
1947-1951	14.7	Return to Normalcy
1952-1954	19.3	Korean Conflict Mobilization
1955-1960	16.7	Eisenhower Stability
1961-1968	18.9	Great Society Influences
1969-1984	21.2	Social Security and Entitlement Influences

Source: U.S. Bureau of the Census, *Statistical Abstract of the United States* (Washington, D.C.: U.S. Government Printing Office, 1985); U.S. Bureau of the Census, *Historical Statistics of the United States, Colonial Times to 1970* (Washington, D.C.: U.S. Government Printing Office, 1975).

to identify their correspondence with behavior that was predicted on the basis of ideological predisposition. All other things being equal, it is expected that average outlays as a percentage of gross national product would be higher and grow at a faster pace during identified liberal periods than during periods said to be dominated by conservative thought. Data displayed in Table 1 provide some justification for the view that actual budget outputs were associated with the prevailing ideology of the time.

The conservative period 1921 to 1933 was marked by national spending that averaged 4.9 percent of GNP. This level of expenditure is consistent with the conservative view of the desirability of a minimal public sector. Outlays increased to 9.8 percent of GNP during the period 1934 to

1941, when Franklin D. Roosevelt was able to implement his New Deal programs. Roosevelt's administration reflected a philosophy more acceptable to an active public sector than the administration of Herbert Hoover. Roosevelt's more flexible view of government led to the creation of a new line item in the 1934 budget, "Recovery and Relief." This new category and new approach of government was created in an effort to deal with the problems of society. It accounted for 60 percent of the entire budget in 1934 and resulted in an 84 percent increase in total expenditures from the 1933 level.

The external shock of the Great Depression did not by itself result in increased spending. Political philosophy of the leader appears to be more relevant in determining budget outputs than environmental conditions given that virtually the same conditions confronted President Hoover (between October 1929 and January 1932) as those conditions that confronted President Roosevelt in the post-1932 era. Hoover, however, did not attempt to initiate programs that would address the problems resulting from the economic depression. These programs were initiated by Roosevelt. As a result of this inaction, Hoover and the Republican party have commonly been associated with conservatism and a reluctance to change the existing order of relationships.[7] The Democratic party and the liberal perspective of Roosevelt became associated with a greater willingness to seek change and a willingness to intervene in the private marketplace to ensure economic prosperity.

Under the leadership of Franklin Roosevelt, federal spending levels as a percentage of gross national product doubled to 9.8 percent from the 1921–33 period. This doubling of aggregate spending appears to be the result of the political perspective of its leader, Franklin Roosevelt. The view that government had a responsibility to intervene in the private economy and that government could alleviate economic problems of the day contrasted sharply with the classical liberal view of Herbert Hoover.

It is obvious from Table 1 that World War II dramatically altered the demands placed upon government. Between 1942 and 1946, government spending exploded. As a result of the war, average outlays as a percentage of GNP grew to 35.7 percent. This phenomenal growth was virtually unprecedented yet consistent with the historical pattern in the United States in which wars have an immense impact on government spending.

Following World War II, government spending fell but remained significantly higher than the levels that had existed prior to the war. This is consistent with the thesis of David and Attiat Ott, who found that large expansions of federal spending occurred during the War of 1812, the Civil War, World War I, and World War II. With the return of peace, these authors found, expenditures fall but never fall all the way down to prewar levels. This was largely attributed to interest on debt accumulated during the war and veterans' expenses.[8]

The pattern of war expenditures producing higher aggregate federal spending levels is also observable in the 1952–54 period. An increase in expenditures did result from the Korean War, yet the increase in no way approximated the expansion that occurred in World War II. Due to the huge impact of war, it is virtually impossible in these periods to identify possible policy impacts of ideology. The need to expand spending in time of war appears to be a factor independent of ideology. It should be noted, however, that major American wars of the twentieth century coincided with the administrations of liberal Democratic presidents.

The Kennedy-Johnson era of 1961 to 1968 produced significantly higher levels of social spending than experienced in the Eisenhower period. National outlays as a percentage of GNP increased to 18.9 percent in the Kennedy-Johnson period. The war in Vietnam produced increases in defense spending; however, Johnson's domestic programs accounted for the lion's share of the expenditure growth. This can be observed through analysis of defense spending as a proportion of total spending. In 1963 (prior to major American involvement in Vietnam), defense spending as a proportion of total spending was 56.9 percent. This proportion shrank to 45 percent in 1968 at the height of the war.[9] This is only one indication that the war in Vietnam was different from other wars in the nation's history. These figures also demonstrate that the war should not be blamed for the increases in the aggregate federal spending that marked the Johnson administration.

On the basis of ideology one would have expected a contraction of government expenditures once the liberal Johnson left office and was replaced by the more conservative Nixon. This, however, did not occur. Spending increased in the post-Johnson period. A number of factors are cited to explain this apparent anomaly. Some of the increase can be explained by a liberal Congress and the weakening of Nixon as a result of the Watergate scandal. These factors, however, do not explain the growth of spending that occurred between 1980 and 1986, when the United States Senate was controlled by the Republican party and Ronald Reagan enjoyed tremendous popularity.

Increasing expenditure levels have occurred even under the conservative Reagan administration. This appears to contradict earlier data linking the ideology of administrations to budget outputs. Allen Schick provides some explanations for the increase in aggregate spending that has occurred in the conservative Reagan period.[10] First, government spending automatically increases as a result of a number of large entitlement programs indexed to the rate of inflation. Social security is a prime example of a government entitlement program that automatically promoted spending, regardless of executive action. Social security and other social insurance programs grew exponentially between 1954 and 1980.[11]

A second factor explaining the growth of expenditures during the Reagan administration was the deficit. Interest payments on the public debt accounted for $179 billion in

1985, more than 10 percent of total federal expenditures.[12] These payments have increased dramatically because of the more than $1 trillion that have been added to the national debt since the Kemp-Roth tax cut of 1981.

Finally, increased defense expenditures have contributed to the growth of total spending in the Reagan administration. In 1975, national defense spending totaled $86.6 billion. By 1987, the defense budget grew to $290 billion.[13] Secretary of Defense Casper Weinberger sought $1.46 trillion in 1981 for his five-year defense spending plan. David Stockman, head of Reagan's Office of Management and Budgets, noted that Weinberger, previously known as "Cap the Knife" for his cutting of expenditures, had been transformed into "Cap the Shovel" as a result of his requested increases in spending.[14]

Although government spending as a whole did not decline in the Reagan administration, there is ample evidence of the influence of conservative thinking on post-1982 budget outputs. John Palmer and Isabel Sawhill of the Urban Institute stated that budgetary change has been significant in the Reagan administration, producing large cuts in marginal tax rates, cuts in social programs, and increases in defense spending. Changes that have occurred, according to these authors, have resulted in the largest redirection of public purposes since 1932.[15]

State Level

The United States is by no means a homogeneous society. Differences abound between different states, regions, ethnic groups, cultures, philosophies, and social classes. Cultural diversity in the United States has long been recognized. Daniel Elazar stated that in reality there are three separate and distinct cultures in the United States: a traditional culture, a moralistic culture, and an individualistic culture.[16] Elazar's insights provide an explanation for philosophical and policy differences that exist in the nation.

Ideological variation between states can be identified through methods such as a comparison of voting records of representatives to the U.S. Congress. These voting records are used to grossly measure a state's ideological preferences. Scores assigned by the Americans for Democratic Action (ADA) are utilized here. ADA scores representing every congressional district in a state in addition to the ADA scores of the state's two senators were averaged to determine an "ideology score" for each of the 50 states. The following formula is employed to determine "ideology scores" of the respective states:

$$\frac{\text{Sum of Congressional District plus Senatorial ADA Scores}}{N}$$

Table 2 describes "ideology scores," per capita general expenditures, and per capita total taxes for the nation's 50 states. It is expected that ideology scores will be associated with the two budget variables described in Table 2. States identified (by their ideology scores) as conservative are expected to be associated with lower taxes and lower levels of spending than states identified (by their ideology scores) as liberal. The predicted associations were discovered when statistical techniques were employed.[17] The bivariate correlations that were discovered represent a more definitive explanation of the relationship that exists between ideology and budget outputs than relationships previously described at the international or national level. The most detailed investigation of the relationships between ideology and budget is carried out at the local level.

Local Level

The influence of political ideology on budgeting is also discovered at the local level. It would be unrealistic to assume that all cities are guided by an identical set of values and political predispositions. Intuitively, one would imagine that

Table 2
ADA Scores and Budget Outputs, 1980

State	Ideology Score	Per Capita Gen. Exp.	Per Capita Total Taxes
Alabama	22	504	121
Alaska	44	1361	400
Arizona	22	805	281
Arkansas	31	428	111
California	48	1016	477
Colorado	47	829	372
Connecticut	72	676	416
Delaware	48	637	155
Florida	33	717	210
Georgia	23	593	216
Hawaii	67	437	193
Idaho	6	585	189
Illinois	39	756	378
Indiana	35	592	235
Iowa	45	739	300
Kansas	22	697	305
Kentucky	36	435	142
Louisiana	23	588	185
Maine	42	720	221
Maryland	62	916	366
Massachusetts	78	839	498
Michigan	61	843	339
Minnesota	52	946	275
Mississippi	17	531	117
Missouri	44	575	271
Montana	54	709	343
Nebraska	33	761	387
Nevada	20	848	296
New Hampshire	34	571	355
New Jersey	66	876	513
New Mexico	17	591	111
New York	59	1368	669
North Carolina	26	592	151
North Dakota	33	638	228
Ohio	40	729	297
Oklahoma	29	537	181
Oregon	48	803	352
Pennsylvania	43	645	293
Rhode Island	68	564	314
South Carolina	30	430	125
South Dakota	30	565	337
Tennessee	35	550	195
Texas	22	599	241
Utah	17	595	203
Vermont	70	521	311
Virginia	21	599	265
Washington	69	729	219
West Virginia	54	446	130
Wisconsin	57	891	281
Wyoming	15	888	364

Source: U.S. Bureau of Census, *County and City Data Book, 1983*; Michael Barone and Grant Ojifusa, *The Almanac of American Politics, 1983*.

the political views of people in one city would differ from the political views of people in other jurisdictions. Cities differ in regard to other characteristics, such as age, population mix, dominant political party, tradition of professionalism or patronage-based politics, and mix of industrial, agricultural, and commercial development. Daniel Elazar stated that different regions of the country and different cities within the nation could be characterized by a distinctive culture. The three cultures were characterized as moralistic, traditional, or individualistic. The culture present in a city such as Dallas was found by Elazar to differ significantly from the culture of a city such as New York. Cultural and philosophical differences between Dallas and New York provide a philosophical justification for differences discovered in public policy outputs.

CONSERVATIVE DALLAS

Common perceptions exist in regard to the degree of "liberalism" or "conservatism" that exists in a jurisdiction. Dallas is perceived as a city thoroughly dominated by an ethic of conservatism. The assassination of President Kennedy in Dallas is only one factor contributing to the aura of conservatism that is associated with the city. Reese McGee, former head of sociology at the University of Mississippi, claimed that barring the state of Mississippi, the assassination of President Kennedy was most likely to have taken place in Dallas for the following reasons: (1) the absolutist nature of local thought, (2) the institutionalization of personalized violence, (3) the proliferation of firearms and the habit of carrying them, (4) the political respectability of the radical right, and (5) the nonexistence, publicly, of the radical left.[18]

Several notorious events illustrate Dallas's antipathy toward liberal politics and liberal politicians in general. These events included the jeering of Lyndon Johnson when he was senator from Texas, the denigration of Adlai Stevenson when he was the ambassador to the United Nations, and the assassination of President Kennedy in 1963.[19] Other factors contributing to the conservative image of Dallas include the presence of right-wing organizations, the content of editorials and letters to the editor in local newspapers, a reverence for business, and a conservative voting record by the city's congressional legislators.

Dallas's conservative image is further reinforced by the perception that business interests control the political structure of the city. The most influential of these groups representing business interests is the Dallas Citizens Council, which exercised political power through the organization Citizens Charter Association (CCA). In 1970, this influential body was composed of 250 chief executives of the city's largest business firms. These executives exercised great influence by selecting business-endorsed slates of candidates for the city council and backing them with professional advertising campaigns. Both major newspapers consistently supported the CCA slate, and with rare exception CCA candidates won a majority of seats on the city council.[20]

The dominance of business groups and the conservative image of Dallas in general are claimed to have contributed to the economic vitality of the city. The image of prosperity that characterizes Dallas is totally justified by historical trends. In 1910, the city and county of Dallas had fewer than 100,000 inhabitants and ranked fifty-fifth in population among cities across the nation. According to the 1980 U.S. census, Dallas was the seventh largest city in the nation and growing at a fast rate. This growth began to develop dramatically in the 1940s as a result of the birth of the aircraft industry. Like other communities in the Southwest, Dallas benefited during World War II from large levels of military spending. Unlike other communities, however, Dallas's economy expanded even after the demobilization that followed the war.[21]

A low tax burden contributed to the probusiness aura of Dallas. In 1977 the estimated state and local tax burden for an average-income family of four was 7.4 percent. This burden was considerably lower than the estimated average tax burden of 9 percent in the thirty largest cities in the United States. When the estimated tax burden for families earning over $30,000 a year was considered, Dallas's rate of 7.6 percent compared favorably with the 9.2 percent rate of the thirty largest cities.[22]

The relatively low tax burden for the city of Dallas is consistent with its image of conservatism. Other cities in the United States project a starkly different image. New York is perhaps as synonymous with an ethic of liberalism as Dallas is synonymous with conservatism. The development of this image as well as an investigation of New York's budget outputs will be reviewed and contrasted with the experience of Dallas.

LIBERAL NEW YORK CITY

New York City has long been associated with big spending and profligate social programs. The fiscal crisis of 1975 greatly reinforced this image of a city living beyond its means. The fiscal crisis finally forced the city to adhere to spending patterns that corresponded to the amount of revenue collected. When New York City was no longer able to sell its bonds, it was forced to cut expenditures dramatically. The high levels of public spending were consistent with liberal predispositions favoring an expansive and expensive public sector and had to be altered in a draconian manner after 1975.

New York City's association with liberalism developed as a result of its history of social consciousness dating from the early 1800s.[23] As a port of entry for immigrants, the city has always been aware of the social problems that develop in large population centers. New York's social consciousness resulted in social legislation passed in an effort to alleviate problems of the poor and downtrodden who dwelled within the city.

History of Social Consciousness in New York City

New York City as a port of entry for immigrants was a focal point of poverty, wretchedness, and injustice. The city's concern with social problems became evident by the late nineteenth century, and efforts were initiated to alleviate those problems through legislation. Jacob Riis, a reformer, was active in the battle against the tenements and slums of the city. Through organizations such as the Children's Aid Society, Riis drew attention to the plight of neglected and abandoned children of New York. He applauded the efforts of agencies such as the Society for the Prevention of Cruelty to Children, which attempted to deal with the conditions of children living within the city.[24]

The Gilder Commission was another example of an organization that worked to improve the living conditions of the poor. As early as 1894, the Gilder Commission began working to outlaw rear tenement apartment dwellings in New York. As a result of these efforts, the Tenement Housing Law was passed in 1895. By 1901, a new Tenement House Law was passed providing for light and ventilation in all rooms. This new tenement legislation also specified that no more than 70 percent of a lot be occupied by a structure, buildings were limited to one-half times the width of the street, no room of less than 70 square feet was permitted, and stairs and hallways were to be fireproofed in buildings of five or more stories.

Riis felt that the greed of capital had brought about the wretched conditions that existed in his day. In 1890, he stated that half the world did not care how the other half lived. Those on the top didn't worry about those on the bottom as long as they were able to hold them there. According to Riis, conditions were so bad for the poor that ignoring them became very difficult for the rich: "The discomfort and crowding below were so great, and the consequent upheavals so violent, that it was no longer an easy thing to do."[25] Riis believed that the upper class began to inquire as to "what was the matter" only when the threat of violence became apparent.[26] This history of social legislation laid the foundation for government activity that would address social problems in future generations.

Budget Trends in New York City, 1959-79

To many observers it might seem incongruous that a city with the fabulous wealth of New York could one day face bankruptcy. This, however, did occur in 1975. One must ask how this turn of events came about. An investigation of revenue and expenditure patterns of the city between 1959 and 1979 helps to answer this question.

New York City earned a reputation for high levels of municipal spending long before its fiscal crisis of 1975. Roy Bahl, Alan Campbell, and David Greytak compared New York's per capita expenditures in 1971 with the average per capita expenditures of the ten largest cities in the nation. These authors found that per capita expenditures in New York were consistently higher than their ten-city average. Per capita expenditures in New York City in 1971 were $1,207 compared with an average of $685 in the ten largest cities of the nation.[27]

The situation in which New York found itself did not arise overnight but developed over a period of time. Between fiscal years 1963-64 and 1973-74, expenditures more than tripled, with state and federal aid accounting for much of the increase.[28] The dependence on state and federal aid, however, was not cost-free. Municipal expenditures had to grow in order to qualify for matching federal funds. Growth of

programs also often outstripped the growth of intergovernmental aid. When federal and state aid programs began to
contract, the city was left "holding the bag" of expensive and
expanding program expenditures. The contraction of intergovernmental grant programs put great pressure on the city's
finances and their ability to pay for rapidly increasing
expenditures.

An explosion of spending occurred in the area of social
welfare in the 1960s and 1970s. This increase was congruent
with the liberal image of New York and its corresponding
willingness to help the poor. Between 1959 and 1979 the percentage of total city expenditures allocated to social welfare
functions (included Public Welfare, Education, Health and
Hospitals) expanded from 55 percent of the total city budget
to 70 percent of total expenditures. All other major categories of spending declined as a proportion of total spending
in that period. Changes in proportions of total spending for
each major expenditure category are described in Table 3.

The changes in share of the total budget illustrates New
York's commitment to social welfare functions. Changes in
the city's budget priorities or alterations in spending patterns

Table 3
Proportions of Functional Spending to Total Spending, 1959-79

Year	Social Welfare	Urban Services	Infra-structure	Amenity	Gov't. Admin.
1959	55%	17%	20%	3%	5%
1979	70%	13%	11%	3%	3%

Source: U.S. Department of Commerce, *City Government Finances
1959-60* (Washington, D.C.: U.S. Government Printing Office, 1961);
U.S. Department of Commerce, *City Government Finances 1978-79*
(Washington, D.C.: U.S. Government Printing Office, 1980).

can also be identified for individual agencies. It is clear that some functions, such as Public Welfare, were very successful in securing funding whereas other functions were much less successful. An "index of relative success" can be developed to more clearly identify which functions and agencies fared well in their efforts to secure funding. Winners and losers in the struggle for scarce resources are readily observed through this index of relative success.

Index of Relative Success

An index of relative success describes the remarkable growth of social expenditures that occurred in "liberal" New York between the period of 1959 to 1979. In this period general expenditures grew from approximately $2.1 billion to almost $12 billion. This represented an increase of approximately 471 percent. The expansion of general expenditures. suggests that the liberal city of New York was amenable to increases in overall spending. Spending growth, however, was much faster for individual expenditure categories. For example, public welfare spending increased from approximately $269 million in 1959 to almost $2.9 billion in 1979, representing an expansion of 970 percent.

Both the increase in general expenditures and the increase in individual expenditure categories are used in calculating an index of relative success. This index describes how much faster or slower an individual expenditure category grew compared with the increase in all expenditure categories. The increase in all expenditure categories is represented by the percentage increase in general expenditures. Scores of more than one (1.00) on the index describe growth in individual categories that was faster than the average growth of all expenditures in the city. Scores of less than one (1.00) on the index describe individual spending categories that have grown at a slower pace than the average of all expenditures. For example, an index of relative success of +2.06 can be calculated

Table 4

Relative Success of Individual Governmental Agencies: New York City,
1959-79

Expenditure Category	Score on Index of Relative Success
Public Welfare	2.06
Health	1.28
Corrections	.92
Hospitals	.86
Education	.85
General Public Bldgs.	.75
Sewage	.70
Police	.69
Libraries	.69
Fire	.65
Financial Admin.	.59
Parks and Recreation	.46
Sanitation	.45
General Control	.35
Highways	.13

Source: U.S. Department of Commerce, *City Government Finances*
(Washington, D.C.: U.S. Government Printing Office).

for the public welfare function. This is determined by dividing
the growth of the individual expenditures category by the
growth of general expenditures, or by dividing 970 percent

by 471 percent. From this index one can clearly see that growth of public welfare expenditures was more than twice the pace of growth in all expenditures. Scores of less than one indicate expenditure categories that failed to keep up with the total growth in expenditures. Table 4 describes the uneven growth patterns that existed in functional expenditures for the period 1959 to 1979 in the city of New York. The targeting of expenditures for social welfare functions is again consistent with the image of New York as a big-spending liberal city.

From Table 4 it is readily apparent that increases in total spending for the city of New York were fueled by increased spending in the public welfare function. Liberal concerns for greater equity and social justice may have contributed to this decision to prioritize welfare spending to the detriment of virtually all other groups. A more direct comparison of budgets in New York and Dallas clearly identifies policy differences that exist on the local level between these cities.

COMPARISON OF FISCAL OUTPUTS: NEW YORK AND DALLAS

A great deal of difference can be found when comparing budget outputs of the cities of New York and Dallas. One of these differences relates to the stability of revenue sources in both cities. New York, with its high tax burden, high dependence on intergovernmental aid, and willingness to borrow, possessed a much less stable source of revenue than did the city of Dallas. In the late 1970s most revenue sources actually declined in New York City. New York recognized that high taxes caused businesses and residents to flee the city, further eroding the tax base. New York also faced an environment of stagnant economic growth compared with the economic dynamism of Dallas. Between 1950 and 1970, total employment increased 87.1 percent in the city of Dallas compared with a decline of 2.6 percent in New York. Between 1954

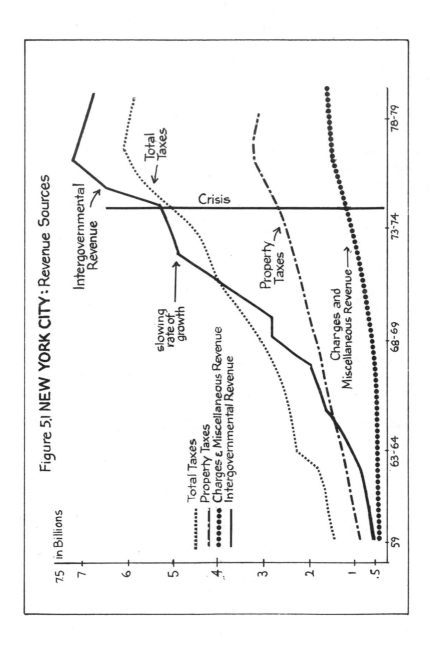

Figure 5.1 NEW YORK CITY: Revenue Sources

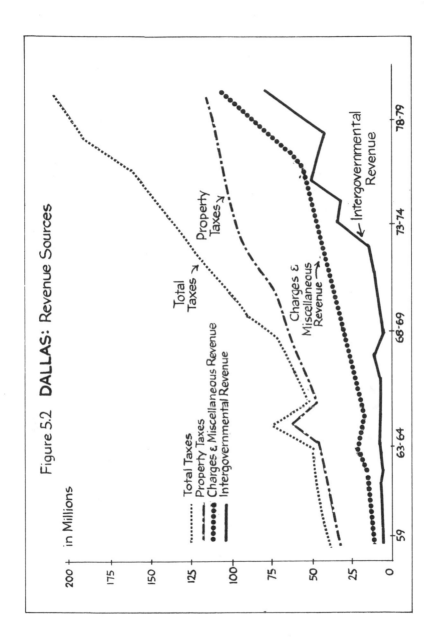

Figure 5.2 **DALLAS:** Revenue Sources

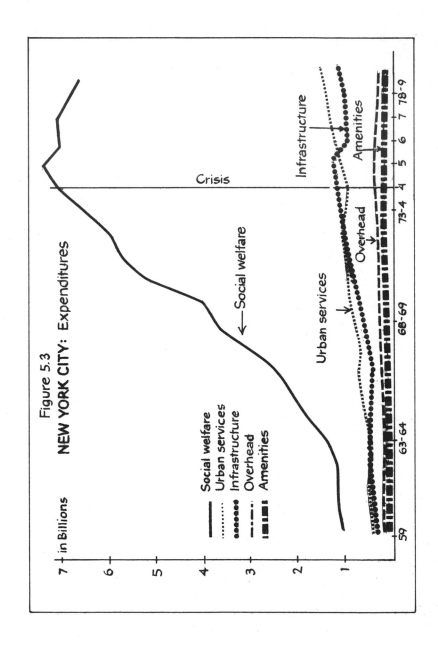

Figure 5.3
NEW YORK CITY: Expenditures

Social welfare
Urban services
Infrastructure
Overhead
Amenities

Crisis

Social welfare

Infrastructure

Amenities

Overhead

Urban services

in Billions

7
6
5
4
3
2
1

59   63-64   68-69   73-4   4   5   6   7   78-9

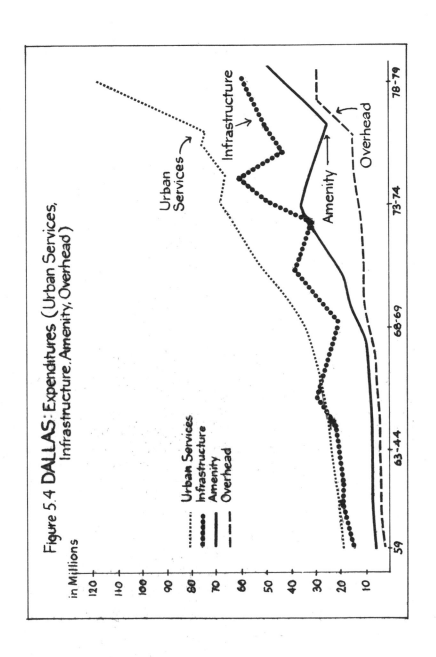

Figure 5.4 DALLAS: Expenditures (Urban Services, Infrastructure, Amenity, Overhead)

and 1972, value added by manufacturing increased 278.1 percent in Dallas compared with 73.6 percent in New York, and retail sales increased by only 66.1 percent in the Big Apple compared with 165.9 percent in the big D.[29]

What has been termed the Laffer curve may have worked to increase total public sector revenues in Dallas. The increase in revenue was attained through an expansion of the economy coinciding with low tax rates. A combination of negative economic factors plus a reduction of intergovernmental aid combined to reduce the amount of revenue available to New York. Trends of revenue growth for both cities are described in Figures 5.1 and 5.2.

Differences between the two cities are also discovered when investigating expenditure patterns. One major difference concerns the number of services assumed by each city. New York City assumed funding responsibilities for 15 governmental functions: education, hospitals, health, public welfare, police, fire, sanitation, highways, sewage, housing, library, parks and recreation, financial administration, general control, and general public buildings. The large number of services assumed by New York is consistent with the liberal view of the desirability of an expansive public sector. This perspective holds that government has a responsibility to deal with problems of society. Because responsibility is willingly accepted, perhaps even sought, by liberals, there would be little sentiment to relegate funding responsibilities to other governmental jurisdictions, such as the county.

In contrast to New York, Dallas assumed funding responsibility for only ten public services. This is consistent with the conservative desire for limited government. "Essential" services were assumed by Dallas; social welfare functions such as education, hospitals, health, public welfare, and housing were considered the responsibility of other governmental jurisdictions.

Figures 5.3 and 5.4 describe expenditure patterns for both cities between 1959 and 1979. Dallas's spending is concentrated in what is viewed as the "essential services" of police, fire, and sanitation. Social welfare spending, as previously discussed, dominated New York's expenditures, accounting for 70 percent of the city's total budget in 1979.

Social welfare spending included spending for the following categories: public welfare, education, health, and hospitals. Urban service expenditures included police, fire, and sanitation; amenity expenditures consisted of library and parks and recreation; infrastructure spending included the categories highway, sewage, and housing; while overhead expenditures were made up of financial administration, general public buildings, and general control.

Ironically, the fiscally conservative budget policies characteristic of the city of Dallas may have allowed for increasing expenditures, whereas the less prudent budgetary practices of New York led to spending cuts. New York's fiscal crisis forced the city to adopt policies that would decrease expenditures. Policies of tax abatement were enacted to stabilize the economic base. This strategy was coupled with significant cuts in social welfare spending, the very category that grew so precipitously during the 1960s and early 1970s. Figures 5.5 and 5.6 describe trends in total expenditures for both New York and Dallas.

It is clear that major budgetary differences exist between New York and Dallas. The liberal city of New York was characterized by higher taxes, higher levels of spending, more functions, and greater reliance on intergovernmental aid. Conversely, the conservative city of Dallas was characterized by lower levels of taxation, lower levels of spending, less dependence on intergovernmental aid, and fewer functions. Specific budget characteristics of both cities are compared in Table 5.

Policy differences believed to result from different ideological perspectives should not be unique to Dallas and New York. If budget outputs are related to differences in philosophical orientation, these differences should also be found

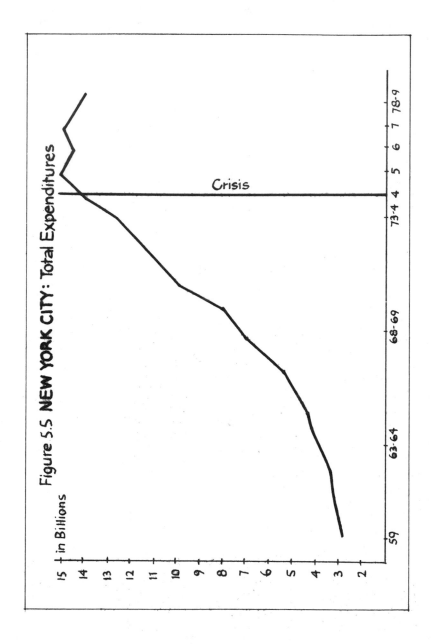

Figure 5.5 NEW YORK CITY: Total Expenditures

Crisis

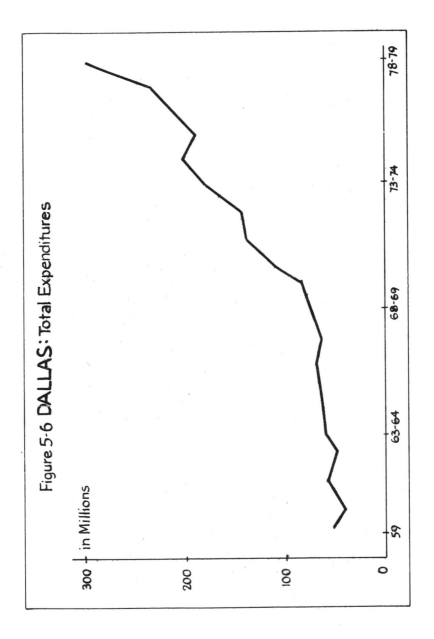

Figure 5-6 DALLAS: Total Expenditures

in Millions

Table 5
Budget Characteristics of New York and Dallas, 1979–80

City	Number of Services	Per Cap. Gen. Exp.	Per Cap. Prop Taxes	Per Cap. Tot Taxes	% Revenue Integov. Aid
N.Y.C.	15	$1,863	$456	$948	47
Dallas	10	$408	$136	$239	17

Source: U.S. Bureau of Census, *City Government Finances, 1979–80* (Washington, D.C.: U.S. Government Printing Office, 1981).

when a larger number of cities are compared. The linkage between philosophical perspective and budget outputs is therefore explored for the 20 largest cities in the United States.

COMPARISON OF BUDGET OUTPUTS: 20 LARGEST CITIES IN THE UNITED STATES

Voting records of representatives of the 20 largest cities in the United States were used to identify the extent of liberal or conservative sentiment of the respective cities. Americans for Democratic Action (ADA) scores of congressional districts from the 20 cities during the period 1971 to 1980 were summed and averaged. These scores are interpreted to represent the ideological predispositions of the cities and ranged from a high of 91 for Baltimore to a low of 7 for Phoenix. Yearly scores of a city were calculated by summing congressional district scores for a city and dividing by the number of districts. For example, there are 16 congressional districts from New York City and two congressional districts that represent the city of Dallas. To calculate New York's score, the individual ADA scores for each of the districts were summed and divided by 16: for Dallas the two district scores were summed and divided by two.

The scores for each of the 20 cities were arrayed and two distinct groups were identified: liberal cities and conservative cities. Liberal cities consisted of cities with average ADA scores ranging from 66 to 91. Baltimore (91), San Francisco (90), Los Angeles (85), New York (80), Cleveland (80), Memphis (79), Boston (77), Detroit (74), Milwaukee (71), Chicago (68), Philadelphia (67), and San Jose (66) represented the cities in the liberal group. Cities in the conservative group included Houston (60), San Diego (51), San Antonio (36), Indianapolis (31), New Orleans (25), Dallas (18), Columbus (13), and Phoenix (7).

A number of assumptions had to be made in order to place cities within ideological groupings. These included the following: (1) Elected congress representatives of a particular municipality reflected the political culture or political ideology of that municipality, and (2) Americans for Democratic Action has accurately identified the ideological posture of legislators through their scoring procedures.

Prior to investigating budget outputs in liberal and conservative groups of cities, problems existing with comparative urban analysis must be discussed. Major problems exist in attempts to compare accurately the budget behaviors among American cities. One of the primary problems relates to the fact that numbers of services are not identical between jurisdictions. Numbers of services assumed by the twenty largest cities in the nation range from a high of 15 in New York to a low of nine for the cities of Memphis, Phoenix, San Diego, and San Jose. Table 6 describes the different services assumed by each city.

Some of the problems of noncomparability in urban analysis can be seen from an inspection of Table 6. For example, it would be difficult to say that Phoenix was twice as efficient in delivering services on the basis of per capita expenditures

Table 6
Numbers of Services Assumed by Cities

Number of Services (20 years)

City	Tot	Ed	Ho	He	PW	Pl	Fr	Sn	Hy	Sw	Hs	Lb	PR	FA	GC	GPB
New York	15	1	1	1	1	1	1	1	1	1	1	1	1	1	1	1
Baltimore	14	1	1	1	0	1	1	1	1	1	1	1	1	1	1	1
San Francisco	14	0	1	1	1	1	1	1	1	1	1	1	1	1	1	1
Boston	13	1	1	0	0	1	1	1	1	1	1	1	1	1	1	1
Philadelphia	13	0	0	1	1	1.	1	1	1	1	1	1	1	1	1	1
Chicago	13	0	1	1	0	1	1	1	1	1	1	1	1	1	1	1
Detroit	13	0	1	1	0	1	1	1	1	1	1	1	1	1	1	1
New Orleans	12	0	0	1	0	1	1	1	1	1	1	1	1	1	1	1
Los Angeles	11	0	0	0	0	1	1	1	1	1	1	1	1	1	1	1
San Antonio	10	0	0	0	0	1	1	1	1	1	0	1	1	1	1	1
Cleveland	10	0	0	0	0	1	1	1	1	1	1	0	1	1	1	1
Dallas	10	0	0	0	0	1	1	1	1	1	0	1	1	1	1	1
Houston	10	0	0	0	0	1	1	1	1	1	0	1	1	1	1	1
Milwaukee	10	0	0	0	0	1	1	1	1	1	0	1	1	1	1	1
Indianapolis	8	0	0	0	0	1	1	1	1	1	0	0	1	1	1	0
Columbus	8	0	0	0	0	1	1	1	1	1	0	0	1	1	1	0
Memphis	9	1	0	0	0	1	1	1	1	1	0	0	1	1	1	0
Phoenix	9	0	0	0	0	1	1	1	1	1	0	1	1	1	1	0
San Diego	9	0	0	0	0	1	1	1	1	1	0	1	1	1	1	0
San Jose	9	0	0	0	0	1	1	1	1	1	0	1	1	1	1	0
Totals:		4	6	7	3	20	20	20	20	20	10	16	20	20	20	14

Key:1 = service; 0 = no service Ed=Education, Ho=Hospitals, He=Health,
PW=Public Welfare, Pl=Police, Fr=Fire, Sn=Sanitation, Hy=Highways, Sw=Sewage,
Hs=Housing, Lb=Library, PR=Parks & Recreation, FA=Financial Administration,
GC=General Control, GPB=General Public Buildings

that were half the level of those found in New York. This would be highly misleading if one ignored the fact that New York provided many more services than the city of Phoenix. To fairly compare budget outputs such as taxes and expenditures, it is necessary to make sure that both budgets represent the same thing. Adjusting for the budgetary impacts of noncomparable services is one way to ensure that "apples" and "oranges" are not being compared. General problems of comparing city budgets and specific recommendations for making comparisons feasible are discussed in order to understand why adjustments are necessary.

Problems of Comparing City Budgets

Myriad overlapping local jurisdictions and fuzzy areas of responsibility have created a situation whereby a great deal of comparative urban analysis simply does not exist. In 1962, there were over 91,000 local governments, including 3,043 counties; 17,997 municipalities; 34,678 school districts; and approximately 36,000 townships, villages, and assorted special districts.[30] These different types of governments varied in terms of service responsibility and opportunity to tax. For example, we know that New York City assumed responsibilities for a larger number of services than did cities such as Dallas and Phoenix. Astrid E. Merget stated that expenditure patterns across cities were especially tricky to interpret. She stated that even within a single state, responsibilities across cities are often incomparable. In order to address this problem, Merget recommended comparison of only comparable functions between cities.[31]

It may be possible to compare revenue and expenditure levels of different cities by accounting for the influence of "extra" services. For example, it would make no sense to compare per capita general expenditures between cities that assumed responsibilities for different numbers of services. One would naturally expect that expenditures would be higher in cities that provided a wider range of services. This would not mean that comparable costs were higher in those cities or that those cities were less efficient in provision of services. Individual costs for comparable services may indeed be lower in the city assuming high numbers of services. County and school district costs may have to be added to some cities (low service-assuming city) in order to compare fairly the total expenditure levels between cities assuming responsibility for different numbers of functions. Costs can also be compared by adjusting for or subtracting out the influences of the noncomparable, "extra" services. Means of comparing revenue and expenditure levels through adjusting for the effect of noncomparable services are explained through the application of the following decision rules:

1. *General expenditures.* To make general expenditures comparable between cities, expenditures for noncomparable functions such as education, public welfare, health and hospitals, and housing are to be subtracted from general expenditures in cities assuming these "extra" functions.

2. *Intergovernmental revenue.* In cities assuming more than minimal levels of services, intergovernmental revenue earmarked for "extra" services are identified and subtracted from total aid received by state and federal sources.

3. *Charges and miscellaneous revenue.* Charges obtained from "extra" services are identified and subtracted from the total charges and miscellaneous revenues.

4. *Long-term debt.* Debt assumed for "extra" services are identified and subtracted from the long-term debt of municipalities.

5. *Total taxes.* Expenditures of "extra" services are subtracted from total expenditures; the proportion of city expenses paid by taxes is identified; and this proportion is multiplied by the reduced total expenditure figure. This decision rule assumes that the proportion of total expenditures paid by taxes is constant and will not vary by the level of total expenditures.

6. *General revenues*. The adjusted figure for general revenues is computed by summing the adjusted levels of intergovernmental revenue, charges and miscellaneous revenue, and total taxes.

The foregoing decision rules correct for "extra" services, which are defined as services assumed by some cities but not others. This allows for comparability between cities given that only basic or minimal levels of services are considered. Subtracting out the effects of noncomparable services will provide a gross estimate of how cities compare in terms of basic services. This may not, however, provide a very good perception of the extent of differences that exist between cities. For example, major differences between New York and other cities would probably be underestimated given that the tremendous growth of social spending would be ignored. New York might appear more or less like other cities when only basic services were compared. An alternative strategy not followed here would be to compute county spending for functions such as welfare and add those expenditures to municipal spending in order to bring all cities up to spending levels that include all functions. Per capita expenditures and revenues for the twenty largest cities in the United States were adjusted according to the decision rules delineated earlier. Adjusted budget patterns are now compared between large cities dichtomized on the basis of "conservative" and "liberal" ideologies.

Comparison of Per Capita Budget Variables in Large Cities

Once adjustments are made on the basis of decision rules, budget outputs in large cities can be compared. Adjustments were made in the groups of cities identified as "liberal" or "conservative." Even after the adjustments were made for the many more services assumed by liberal cities, statistically significant differences between "liberal" and "conservative" cities were identified when per capita revenues were compared. General revenues, federal aid, and state aid were all significantly higher in the liberal group of cities.[32]

A number of explanations can be offered as to why liberal cities secured higher levels of per capita intergovernmental revenue, even after adjusting for noncomparable services. The willingness of cities to seek out assistance from other sources of revenue varies between jurisdictions. Conservative cities may have been reluctant to accept federal aid because of the requirement that local governments match some proportion of the federal money. Conservative cities may also have been reluctant to accept outside aid if they feared that the influence of the federal government in local affairs would increase. Deil Wright stated that although it may be politically and economically unwise to turn down federal aid, political leaders were not unaware of restraints placed upon them by federal grants.[33]

Once all adjustments for noncomparable services were made, comparison of spending levels in liberal and conservative cities were made. Given the growth of spending in noncomparable services such as public welfare and education, differences between liberal and conservative cities are likely to be understated. This is true because decision rules subtract out the effects of these expensive services. Spending patterns in essential services are compared in the 20 largest cities in the United States. As one might expect, statistically significant differences between the liberal and conservative groups of cities were discovered even after adjusting for "extra" services. Per capita spending in the aggregate and for specific functions was significantly higher in the liberal group of cities.[34]

Budgetary differences discovered when the groups of liberal and conservative cities were compared are summarized in Table 7. This table identifies revenue and expenditure priorities for each group of cities.

Table 7
Budget Policy Differences: Liberal and Conservative Cities

	Policies Associated with Liberal Cities	Policies Associated with Conservative Cities
Expenditure Outputs	1. Generally higher levels of expenditures	1. Generally lower levels of expenditures
	2. Higher priority to social spending	2. Lower priority to social spending
	3. Lower priority to highway, sewage and other infrastructure spending	3. Higher priority to highway, sewage and other infrastructure spending
Revenue Outputs	1. Greater reliance on progressive income taxes	1. Lower reliance on progressive income taxes
	2. Greater reliance on federal grants	2. Lower reliance on federal grants
	3. Lower reliance on fees or charges	3. Greater reliance on fees or charges

Liberal cities were characterized by higher levels of expenditures, were more likely to assume responsibility for "extra" social services, were more dependent upon intergovernmental revenue, and relied to a lesser extent on fees or charges as a source of revenue than conservative cities. Conservative cities were characterized by lower levels of expenditures, were more likely to assume responsibility for only essential services, were less dependent upon intergovernmental revenue, and relied on fees or charges as a source of revenue to a greater extent than was the practice in liberal cities.

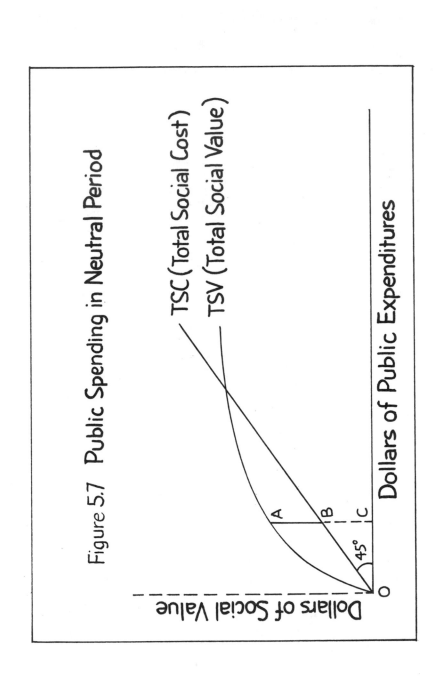

Figure 5.7 Public Spending in Neutral Period

IDEOLOGY AND BUDGET POLICY—
GENERAL GUIDELINES

The data explored at the various levels of government (international, national, state, and local) suggest that public budgetary policy is linked to political sentiment characteristic of jurisdictions. Political perspectives affect interpretation of questions such as what the "proper" size of government should be, and what types of services should be prioritized. Liberals in general tend to be more optimistic about governments' ability to make improvements in the human condition. They are more willing to allow government to try to alleviate conditions of human suffering. In jurisdictions dominated by liberal philosophies or in periods when these philosophies were more dominant, the perceived value of government was enhanced. The greater perceived value placed upon the public sector in turn created an environment for increases in public expenditures.

The economic concept of social value explains how perception of the value of public sector services affects total spending. Figure 5.7 describes how total social value (TSV) of a policy is related to the amount of money spent on the policy. The nature of the TSV curve reflects declining marginal social values at higher levels of public expenditures. The Principle of Maximum Social Gain can be applied to determine appropriate levels of spending.[35] This principle states that expenditure levels depend upon the social value of those expenditures. From Figure 5.7 one can determine the expenditure level as representing the maximum difference between social cost and social value. This is represented by the vertical distance AB. The level of public spending corresponding to this maximum difference between cost and value is represented by OC.

Social value, however, is a dynamic rather than a fixed concept. Because of the ideological influences on the interpretation of social value of the public sector, social value

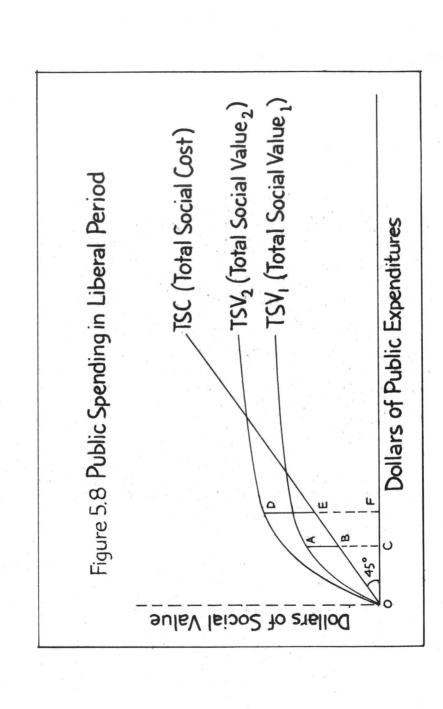

Figure 5.8 Public Spending in Liberal Period

expands or contracts depending upon the period or the juris-diction. For example, in periods when liberal influence was great or in liberal jurisdictions, one would expect to find more positive attitudes toward the public sector and there-fore higher levels of public spending. Technically, this would occur because the value of social goods would be enhanced and the total social value curve would shift upward and to the left. The shifting of this curve reflects the more positive attitude of liberals toward government programs.

Figure 5.8 explains how the shifting of the Total Social Value curve results in higher levels of public expenditures when the Principle of Maximum Social Gain is applied. As the initial Total Social Value (TSV1) curve shifts outward (to TSV2), the maximum difference between social value and social cost increases to DE and spending increases to OF. Spending increases are attributed to the enhanced perception of government, and the higher perceived social value of pub-lic sector spending.

THREAT OF IDEOLOGY TO OBJECTIVITY

This chapter investigated the linkages between ideology and budget outputs. The underlying issue addressed here concerns the question of what should be the role of ideology in the development of public policy. A number of different perspectives deal directly with this issue.

To advocates of governmental responsiveness, public policy alterations based upon ideology are viewed as a positive development. This is perceived as positive because the elec-toral process elects leaders advocating specific philosophies and those philosophies then shape policy. The people are protected from administrative authoritarianism, and power can ultimately be traced to them. Voters, through executive controls, have ultimate authority over nonelected bureaucrats. Ideology reflected in popular politics triumphs over techno-cratic values.

Francis E. Rourke contended that the possibility of bureaucrats becoming a power elite, dominating all governmental decisions, haunted American political life.[36] Bureaucracy was perceived to pose a potential threat to democracy for the following reasons: (1) it could serve as a tool for the enhancement of state domination, (2) it had the potential of encroaching on the liberties and privacy of individuals, and (3) it had exempted itself from the democratic process.[37]

These issues remain a cause of concern, however; the threat ideology poses to objective policymaking must be recognized. Ideological blinders will have an extremely negative influence on society if they prevent policymakers from carrying out objective analysis of fundamental problems. Just as the electoral process is a check on the bureaucracy, the bureaucracy must have enough autonomy to act as a check on elected officials.

Public administrators must deal with the problem of ideologically motivated public sector employees attempting to reshape policy according to their own perspectives. More objective standards and criteria must be developed in order to constrain the power and influence of ideologically motivated political appointees. In the absence of these objective standards, public policies may be continuously held hostage to the vagaries of ideology.

It has long been recognized that good government depends upon the political zeal of appointees as well as the detached expertise of career bureaucrats. Today the balance between these competing values may be shifting in favor of political appointees placed in positions of power on the basis of "correct" ideology. Public administration as a discipline will suffer if the ethos of neutral competence is replaced by the ethos of ideology. Public administration will not be the only casualty of this scenario. The quality of public policy will also decline if objective managerial values are replaced by ideologically motivated values. Chapter 6 discusses objective analysis in the budgetary process and explains how politics as well as ideology can interfere with these rational processes.

NOTES

1. V. O. Key, Jr., "The Lack of a Budgetary Theory," *American Political Science Review* 34 (December 1940): 1137-44.

2. Quoted in Aaron Wildavsky, "Rescuing Policy Analysis from PPBS," *Public Administration Review* 29 (March/April 1969): 189-202.

3. Michael Barone and Grant Ujifusa, eds., *The Almanac of American Politics 1984* (Washington, D.C.: National Journal, 1983).

4. Milton Friedman and Rose Friedman, *Free to Choose* (New York: Avon Books, 1979).

5. Arnold Heidenheimer, Hugh Heclo, and Carolyn Adams, *Comparative Public Policy: The Politics of Social Choice in Europe and America* (New York: St. Martin's Press, 1983).

6. Louis Hartz, *The Liberal Tradition in America* (New York: Harcourt, Brace & World, 1955).

7. Angus Campbell, Phillip Converse, Warren Miller, and Donald Stokes, *The American Voter* (New York: John Wiley & Sons, 1964), p. 111.

8. David Ott and Attiat Ott, *Federal Budget Policy* (Washington, D.C.: The Brookings Institution, 1965), p. 40.

9. *Congressional Quarterly* 27, no. 1 (17 January 1969), p. 91.

10. Allen Schick, "Incremental Budgeting in a Decremental Age," in *Current Issues in Public Administration*, ed. F. Lane (New York: St. Martin's Press, 1986), p. 291.

11. David Stockman, *The Triumph of Politics* (New York: Harper & Row, 1986), p. 409.

12. *Congressional Quarterly* 44, no. 6 (8 February 1986), p. 257.

13. *New York Times*, 16 October 1986.

14. Stockman, *The Triumph of Politics*, p. 278.

15. John Palmer and Isabel Sawhill, eds., *The Reagan Record* (Cambridge, Mass.: Ballinger, 1984), p. 1.

16. Daniel Elazar, *American Federalism: A View from the States* (New York: Thomas Crowell, 1972), p. 93.

17. Bivariate association between states' ADA scores and per capita taxes was statistically significant at the .01 level of confidence. Bivariate association between states' ADA scores and per capita general expenditures was statistically significant at the .10 level of confidence.

18. Warren Leslie, *Dallas Public and Private* (New York: Grossman Publishers, 1964), p. 12.

19. Shirley Achor, *Mexican Americans in a Dallas Barrio* (Tucson: University of Arizona Press, 1978), p. 54.

20. Ibid., p. 61.

21. Ibid., p. 263.

22. Peter Wilson, *The Future of Dallas Capital Plant* (Washington, D.C.: The Urban Institute, 1980), p. 3.

23. First National City Bank, *Profile of a City* (New York: McGraw-Hill, 1972), p. vii.

24. Jacob Riis, *The Children of the Poor* (New York: Garrett Press, 1979), p. vii.

25. Ibid., p. viii.

26. Jacob Riis, *How the Other Half Lives* (New York: Charles Scribner's Sons, 1890), p. 1.

27. The ten largest cities that were investigated are Chicago, Los Angeles, Philadelphia, Detroit, Houston, Baltimore, Dallas, Washington, Cleveland, and New York. See Roy Bahl, Alan Campbell, and David Greytak, *Taxes, Expenditures and the Economic Base: A Case Study of New York City* (New York: Praeger, 1974), pp. 163-74.

28. David Greytak, Donald Phares, and Elaine Morley, *Municipal Output and Performance in New York City* (Lexington, Mass.: D. C. Heath, 1976), p. 25.

29. U.S. Department of Commerce, *County and City Data Book* (Washington, D.C.: U.S. Government Printing Office, 1977).

30. Ira Sharkansky, *The Politics of Taxing and Spending* (New York: Bobbs-Merrill Co., 1969), p. 126.

31. Astrid E. Merget, "The Era of Fiscal Restraint," in *The 1980 Municipal Yearbook* (Washington, D.C.: International City Management Association, 1980), p. 185.

32. Difference of means *t* tests were carried out. Statistically significant differences in general expenditures, total intergovernmental revenue and federal aid were found at the .05 level of significance. Statistically significant differences in state aid were found at the .01 level of significance.

33. Deil Wright, *Understanding Intergovernmental Relations* (North Scituate, Mass.: Duxbury Press, 1978), p. 112.

34. Again, *t* tests were conducted. Statistically significant differences in per capita general expenditures, financial administration, and general public buildings were discovered at the .05 level of significance. Per capita police expenditures differed at the .01 level of significance.

35. Robert Haveman, *The Economics of the Public Sector* (New York: John Wiley & Sons, 1976).

36. Francis E. Rourke, *Bureaucracy, Politics and Public Policy*, 3d ed. (Boston: Little, Brown, 1984), p. 189.

37. Eva Etzioni-Halevy, *Bureaucracy and Democracy—A Political Dilemma* (London: Routledge and Kegan Paul, 1983), pp. 90-91.

6

Rational versus Political Budgeting

One can observe from the previous chapter that on the international, state, and local levels, budget decisions are associated with the political perspective representative of the jurisdiction. Intuitively, this runs counter to the perspective that budgeting is a neutral process of maximizing the utilization of scarce resources. The ideological and political influences on budgeting are apparent, perhaps making the study of budgeting more an art than a science. Factors that run counter to the objective of maximizing the utility of scarce resources come into play. These factors are generally given little attention by traditional economists. Two economists, however, have looked at nontraditional explanations of resource allocation: Anthony Downs and William Niskanen.

Downs described the basic logic of government decision making and concluded that political parties and voters play key roles in the determination of policy. Downs developed a model of democracy based upon the assumption that every democratic government seeks to maximize political support.[1] This model contrasts with the purely economic model, which seeks to maximize social utility for a given amount of scarce resources. The economic model of budgeting has been described by Nobel laureate James Buchanan, as well as other economists.

Buchanan suggested two methods for formulating budgets of the state.[2] The first method, the "organismic" approach, considered the state a separate "person" whose ends were not necessarily directly tied to the ends of individuals in the state. The state as a separate person would act to maximize its own welfare by manipulating government spending and taxation. Spending and taxing would be manipulated so that the marginal gain of further spending in the public sector would be exactly offset by the marginal loss of further taxation. Gains attributed to government spending and losses attributed to taxation were considered in this method to be gains or losses of the state. Effects of spending and taxes on individuals were not considered in this organismic approach. Buchanan's second approach focused upon the desires of individuals in the state. Following this approach, the state was viewed as having no welfare function of its own; it was perceived simply to provide services to individuals.

Downs believed that these two approaches were flawed; the first, or organismic, view of government was based upon the concept of a state that was apart from individual men, and the second, or individualistic, approach did not take coalitions into account. Downs proposed that the primary motive of government was not to maximize a state's welfare or even the welfare of individual citizens. Rather, the primary motive of government was to maximize the number of votes available to them. He stated that "because the government in our model wishes to maximize political support, it carries out those acts of spending which gain the most votes by means of those acts of financing which lose the fewest votes."[3] Downs believed that public sector expenditures would be increased until the vote gain of the last dollar spent on a program was equal to the vote loss of the last dollar collected to finance that program.

Downs claimed that when budgeting, legislators ask whether or not programs are worth the cost in terms of votes gained. Governments are likely to adopt programs if more political support is to be gained than lost from that program. Conversely, if a proposed program expenditure is likely to irritate more voters than it pleases, the party in power will most likely oppose it. Just as private sector firms attempt to maximize profits, Downs believed that elected government leaders try to maximize votes.[4] If we accept these insights, then we must conclude that principles of economic rationality are not of primary importance in public sector budgeting.

William Niskanen also developed a model that differs from the perspective of economic efficiency in the allocation of public sector resources. Niskanen, a member of the Council of Economic Advisers in the Reagan administration, postulated that bureaucrats seek to maximize the size of their agencies. Bureaucrats are said to be concerned with organizational factors such as the size of their salaries, the perquisites of their offices, the reputation of their agencies, and the amount of power they possess. Because these factors are related to the size of bureaucratic agencies, activities that foster agency expansion are given priority. Bureaucrats will compete with other bureaucrats for funds in an effort to increase agency size.[5] This bureaucratic competition in the public sector replaces market competititon of the private sector.

Niskanen noted that the bureaucrat does not necessarily wish to increase expenditures for reasons of personal power and prestige. It is natural for bureaucrats to feel that their work is important and that the country would benefit from increased funding in their agencies. Military personnel probably think that the nation's general good would be served by more defense spending, just as workers for the Department of Housing and Urban Development probably think that too much of our housing stock is substandard and more money should be spent to create better housing. If public sector

workers did not think their job was important and in need of
more generous support, they conceivably would be quite
frustrated, unmotivated, and unproductive.

TRADITIONAL ECONOMIC EXPLANATION
OF RESOURCE ALLOCATION

The concept of marginal returns to satisfaction is central
to the economic view of how to allocate resources between
different functions. The great English economist of the first
half of the twentieth century, A. C. Pigou, noted that just as
an individual will get more satisfaction from his income by
maintaining a certain balance between different types of
expenditures, so will a community, through its government,
maximize satisfaction. Pigou felt that resources should be
distributed among different uses so that the marginal returns
of satisfaction would be the same for all uses.

The concept of marginal utility comes into play in this
analysis. If the government is spending very little on the public good (such as defense), the utility or usefulness of the last
dollar spent in that area is high. If, however, the government
is spending huge sums on the public good (defense), then the
added benefit or usefulness of the last dollar spent in that
area will be lower. The marginal gain or usefulness of the last
dollar spent therefore depends upon the concept of need,
which relates to how much has already been spent for the
service. For example, the need for and the added benefit to
society of a ten-thousandth nuclear bomb is significantly less
than the benefit attributed to the first nuclear weapon. When
additional benefits for a public good (such as defense) fall to
a level that is below the additional benefit attributed to
another public good (for example, cancer research), it is more
efficient for society to allocate money to the public good
with the higher benefit. In this manner marginal returns to
satisfaction are maximized according to principles of economic optimization. Pigou stated that "expenditures should

be distributed between battleships and poor relief in such ways that the last shilling devoted to each of them yields the same real return."[6] Pigou believed that this would optimize the allocation of scarce public resources.

The economic view of budgeting has not been universally accepted. V. O. Key, Jr. believed that budgeting was more of a political than an economic phenomenon. He stated that use of public funds really resolved itself into a matter of value preferences between ends lacking a common denominator. Furthermore, he believed that attempts to neutrally determine values of public services may be fruitless because of the influence of pressure groups and the role of clientele groups in determining allocations.[7] The political view of budgeting being influenced by values was reiterated by William Gorham in testimony before the Joint Economic Committee in 1967. Gorham reiterated that "grand decisions—how much health, how much education, how much welfare, and which groups in the population should benefit" were "questions of value judgments and politics."[8] It was believed that quantitative analysis could not really address these value issues. The critics of the economic perspective of budgeting raise interesting points but have not totally prevented rational techniques of budgeting from being developed.

Rational Budgeting Techniques

Verne Lewis discussed consideration of rational methods of budgeting through the applicability of two methods of analysis. The first is marginal analysis, which was also discussed by Pigou. Lewis contended that because of the phenomenon of diminishing benefits linked to added expenditures to a function (concept of marginal utility), analysis must take place at or near the margin. The issue therefore was not whether one function was more important than another but whether to last dollar spent on one function was a greater benefit to society than the last dollar spent on another.[9]

As suggested by the marginal utility theory, maximum returns of expenditures are obtained when expenditures are distributed among different purposes in such a way that the last dollar spent for each function yields the same real return. Pigou's recommendations therefore lead to analysis of the benefits of increments or analysis at the margin.

The second method described by Lewis refers to the need to evaluate relative effectiveness in achieving a common objective. In this analysis Lewis borrows extensively from the insights expressed by V. O. Key. Lewis claimed that the relative value of different functions, such as defense or health, could not be compared. For comparative purposes it was necessary for alternatives to have a common objective. For example, a number of items can be identified as contributions to a common cause, such as winning a war. One can conceivably compare the relative values of bazookas, hand grenades, and k-rations in terms of their utility toward the common military objective of defeating the enemy.[10] One, however, could not compare the relative value of spending on defense with the relative value of spending on health, education, or housing.

Lewis outlined a number of specific techniques that were perceived to increase rationality in the budgetary process.

1. *Open-end budgeting.* In this technique single estimates are submitted by lower-ranking officials for whatever amount the officials decide to recommend. No limit is placed on requests. Subordinate officials (who are assumed to possess more technical knowledge concerning how money should be spent) provide input. Superiors provide oversight and are not required to accept requested amounts.

2. *Fixed-ceiling budgeting.* Under this plan, a fixed ceiling is established in advance. This plan reduces the likelihood that additional items will be placed on a budget and increases the likelihood that the relative merits of budget functions will be considered at the executive level.

3. *Workload measurement and unit costing budgets.* Cost for accomplishing specific levels of work is calculated. Work

that contributes to the agency's function is identified. Units of work such as numbers of letters typed, miles of highway paved, and number of purchase orders processed are examples of typical workload measures. This type of budgeting focuses upon levels of output or levels of performance and has also been called "performance budgeting."

Performance budgets measure not only the amount of money expended but also what was accomplished in terms of concrete outputs. Performance budgeting is said to be accountable because this technique of budgeting traces what is received for money spent, rather than merely accounting for how much money was spent. Problems nevertheless exist with this type of budgeting.

One such problem is the fact that the tasks of a public agency may not be easily measured. This is true if an agency mission is stated in very broad terms, such as to "eliminate poverty" or to "provide a strong defense." Another problem of performance budgeting relates to its inability to measure quality of work. For example, one can quantify the number of letters coming out of a congressional office, but it is more difficult to measure how well those letters actually addressed the concerns of citizens. Similarly, one can measure the number of claims processed by an unemployment office; yet it is more difficult to quantify the equity and quality of service that is being delivered to unemployed recipients. Unit costing techniques therefore have some merit, but the advantages to these techniques must be qualified.

4. *Increase-decrease analysis*. This budgetary procedure requires identification of alterations in budget items (increases and decreases) from one period to another. Special explanations for changes in line items may be provided. Major advantages of this type of analysis include the facts that it is relatively simple to perform and relatively simple for readers to analyze. Defenders of this technique find that the sheer mass of work involved in reviewing budget estimates precludes examination of every detail for every year. Defenders of

increase-decrease analysis also claim that conditions do not change so rapidly that they necessitate budget issues to be rehashed every year. A good deal of stability is said to be present in budgets; therefore, careful examination of only a relatively small number of items is required. This type of budgeting is very similar to "incremental" budgeting. Incremental budgeting is justified on the basis of its practicality in light of limitations of time, money, and cognitive abilities. A primary criticism of this type of budgeting is that it accepts the status quo, or past allocational decisions, without a careful review of present utility.

5. *Priority listing budgets*. In this method of budgeting, subordinates are required to indicate priorities of items within their budget requests to assist reviewers in determining budget allocations. Implicit in this analysis is the assumption that efficiency will result when the least important elements of a program are eliminated and the most important retained. This is essentially the strategy that is followed in zero-base budgeting.

ZBB was developed at Texas Instruments in 1969 and first adopted in government by former Georgia governor Jimmy Carter for preparation of his fiscal 1973 budget. Peter Pyhrr stated that there were four basic steps to the zero-base approch to budgeting: (1) identify "decision-units," (2) analyze each decision unit in a decision package, (3) evaluate and rank all decision packages, and (4) prepare the operating budget.[11]

Pyhrr stated that "meaningful elements" of each organization must be isolated for analysis. Those meaningful elements were termed decision units. For example, expenditures of a city's Department of Parks and Recreation might be investigated for three meaningful elements: parks, adult recreation, and children's recreation. Decisions in each of these subdivisions were then prioritized and budget decisions for the entire Parks and Recreation Department were formulated.

The second component of ZBB, the "decision packages," were said to be the building blocks for the zero-base concept.

These packages serve to facilitate evaluation and priority setting. In developing the decision packages, different levels of effort are identified. For example, in each of the three decision units previously mentioned (parks, adult recreation, and children's recreation), three levels of effort can be identified. Usually these levels include a reduced level of funding (such as 80 percent of the previous year's funding), an expanded level of funding (such as 120 percent of the previous year's funding), and the same level of funding as the prior year. Each service level denotes a "package" with the reduced level (80 percent of last year's spending) describing the first package of three levels of spending or the first of three packages (1 of 3); the same level of spending (100 percent of last year's spending) represents the second package or second level of spending (2 of 3), and the expanded level (120 percent of last year's spending) represents all the packages of the decision unit (3 of 3). Each unit specifies work to be accomplished for each of the three levels of funding. For example, in the parks component of the Department of Parks and Recreation, lower levels of funding (80 percent of the prior year's spending) may result in less frequent lawn and shrub care, whereas increased funding (120 percent of last year's spending) may result in more plants and improved maintenance. Similarly, the expected results of different funding levels (80, 100, and 120 percent) are denoted for the adult and children's recreation components of the Department of Parks and Recreation.

The ranking process establishes clear priorities in both individual decision units and the department as a whole. Ranking priorities at the departmental level is essential to the process of ZBB. For example, if the head of the Department of Parks and Recreation believed that the most important decision unit under his or her supervision was children's recreation and the least essential was the parks subdivision, a ranking displayed in Table 8 could be carried out.

Priorities can also be established within individual decision units, which are subunits of the entire organization. For

Table 8

Ranking of Decision Units for the Department of Parks and Recreation

Rank	Decision Package	Incremental Cost	Total Cost
1	Child. Rec. 1 of 3	$200,000	$200,000
2	Child. Rec. 2 of 3	$100,000	$300,000
3	Child. Rec. 3 of 3	$100,000	$400,000
4	Adult Rec. 1 of 3	$200,000	$600,000
5	Adult Rec. 2 of 3	$100,000	$700,000
6	Parks 1 of 3	$200,000	$900,000
7	Adult Rec. 3 of 3	$100,000	$1,000,000
8	Parks 2 of 3	$100,000	$1,100,000
9	Parks 3 of 3	$100,000	$1,200,000

example, it might be determined that within the children's recreation decision unit, kiddie swimming, finger painting, and playground are the main activities. Three levels for each of these activities (80, 100, and 120 percent) can be identified, resulting in nine "decision packages." Decision packages can then be ranked in such a manner that higher-priority activities (perhaps swimming) would receive money before less essential activities such as finger painting. Zero-base budgeting, however, does not remove politics from budgeting. Political pressures can be applied to place certain activities in higher-priority rankings. ZBB does succeed in providing managers with a methodology for identifying and funding some activities considered to be of higher priority than others.

6. *Line-by-item control.* Approval of individual line items of expenditure is a common budgetary technique. Equipment purchases, additions to staff, travel, phone bills, and overhead, such as the cost of electricity, are types of items that are often subject to this type of budget control. An

advantage of this method of control is that changes from previous allocations are easily discovered. Spending is not directly linked to programs or broad goals. Because broad program goals are not debated, budget conflicts are likely to be less divisive for agencies. One problem with this technique, however, is that it does not lend itself to systematic consideration of the relative merits of different programs but instead considers spending from the narrower perspective of the cost of individual items.[12]

Other rational techniques not specifically discussed by Lewis include management by objective (MBO) and planning-programming budgeting (PPB). Management by objective is a technique that focuses upon establishment and attainment of concrete objectives. MBO is said to involve three main activities: goal setting, participation, and feedback.[13] Advocates of MBO stress the role of participation in the budget process. MBO does not rely upon classical management theory but is perceived to be rooted in the theories of organizational humanism expounded by management theorists such as Douglas McGregor. In MBO, organizational goals and objectives are set through the participation of organizational members. Organizational members actively partake in the establishment of the group's goals and objectives. This makes participants feel that the goals are legitimate and should increase support for those goals. Through the process of participation it is believed that organization members will have greater dedication and allegiance to the goals of the organization. Jean-Jacques Rousseau's belief that citizen participation helps to legitimize the state provides some justification for the view that participation of all members is healthy for an organization, whether it be the government as a whole or individual workers in an agency. The increased participation inherent in MBO is believed to lead to higher levels of individual motivation, more flexibility, higher performance levels, and greater job satisfaction.[14]

Critics of MBO claim that the technique led to increased

discussion of objectives and decreased amounts of time available to accomplish objectives. The increased paperwork that accompanies MBO procedures was also considered a negative factor. Detractors further claimed that MBO could not be applied to the public sector because objectives in the public sector were stated too ambiguously for accountability to be determined.

Planning-programming budgeting (PPB) is a technique that initially offered great promise to enhance rationality in the budgetary process. For various reasons the promise of PPB was never fulfilled and it is largely discredited today. Planning-programming budgeting was specifically aimed at improving planning prior to the allocation of expenditures and making entire programs rather than specific items or departments the central focus of budget making. PPB is still used in formulating military budgets. In this process, more long-range planning is employed and specific programs are analyzed. In theory, PPB employs sophisticated quantitative techniques in order to judge the relative contributions of various programs (such as missiles and submarines) to the achievement of larger objectives.

Problems of the Rational Perspective

Critics of PPB, such as Aaron Wildavsky, claimed that PPB (which used the logic of systems analysis to increase rationality) was actually too complex for the vast majority of decision makers. Wildavsky stated that no one really knew how to implement PPB, that it produced mountains of useless information, that it suppressed errors, and that it intimidated older managers who did not possess quantitative skills.[15]

Other analysts agree with Wildavsky in his view that many of the rational techniques of analysis were impractical and did not produce better decisions. David Braybrooke and Charles Lindblom stated that an ideal way of making policy was to choose among alternatives after careful and complete study of all possible outcomes. This method of problem solving was similar to what is termed the "synoptic" method. This method was said to be beneficial in regard to its comprehensiveness and objectivity. However, it was perceived to be impractical for a number of reasons. First, conceptual problems such as the inability to prioritize values existed. Second, practical problems such as limitations of time, money, and cognitive abilities of decision makers constrained decision making. The cognitive model provided recommendations for how policy should be made, but it failed to provide details of the process by which rational policy would develop. Lack of a specific methodology for the synoptic method was perceived as a major flaw.[16]

Other problems exist in attempting to apply the synoptic method to the public sector. Ludwig von Mises contended that there was no definitive means of calculating the relative usefulness of government activity. According to Mises, the usefulness of public sector activity could not be priced because the activities of the public sector did not have a price in the free market.[17] This perspective is countered by others such as Charles Tiebout, who claimed that the mix of taxes and services provided by government jurisdictions allowed for a true market test. In Tiebout's model, individuals choose to live in certain jurisdictions based on the mix of price they had to pay for services (taxes) and the product received (actual services delivered). "Citizen voters" were viewed to make rational choices concerning where they desired to live. These choices are said to be analogous to consumer choices for products made in the private sector.[18] Tiebout's model contradicted the more traditional view of economists who maintained that no "market-type" solution existed to determine levels of public expenditure.[19]

In the absence of a market-type solution of allocations, or economically rational solutions, one must conclude that political dynamics should be considered when trying to explain public sector resource allocations. Individual desires of legislators, organizational desires of bureaucrats, and other political factors should be analyzed in order to more fully understand budgeting in the public sector.

THE POLITICAL PERSPECTIVE OF BUDGETING

Political factors and ideological biases undoubtedly affect analysis of budgets and other public policies. Carol Weiss noted that policy research was not neutral but was likely to be motivated by nonrational factors "for reasons of interest, ideology, or intellect." Weiss concluded that these factors led researchers to take positions that "research is not likely to shake."[20] In cases such as this, research is used only as ammunition for decision makers who have made up their minds prior to investigating the issues.

Aaron Wildavsky concurred with Weiss and further postulated that programs could not really be presented on their merits alone because of the lack of agreement in regard to what was considered meritorious. Wildavsky claimed that as a result of this lack of consensus, politics rather than prescriptive models would determine budget allocations.[21] Normative theories of budgeting were not possible in a democracy, according to Wildavsky, because differences of opinion and different value judgments would always be present. Rigid budget prescriptions were said to be more applicable to totalitarian regimes where dissent could be suppressed. Dissent is protected in democratic societies, so allocations and policy in general are perceived to be the result of political conflicts.[22] Policy is not viewed as the result of an applied formula but is continually changing based upon public opinion and the ever-changing powers of interest groups.

The political perspective of policymaking is enunciated in the "group theory" of policymaking.[23] According to this model, politics is viewed as a struggle among groups who vie with each other to influence public policy. Policy in this model is determined by the struggle between interest groups who fight to have their own preferences adopted. Equilibrium is reached through the balancing of the relative strengths of competing groups. Wildavsky further explained how the political process affected budgetary policy:

The size and shape of the budget is a matter of serious contention in our political life. Presidents, political parties, administrators, Congressmen, interest groups, and interested citizens vie with one another to have their preferences recorded in the budget. The victories and defeats, the compromises and bargains, the realms of agreement and the sphere of conflict in regard to the role of the national government in our society all appear in the budget. In the most integral sense, the budget lies at the heart of the political process.[24]

One can readily see the intergroup competition that exists in our society. Policies are more likely to be approved when they have the support of a broad coalition than when they serve only a narrow constituency. Narrow interests generally prevail only when the issue is of little concern to other powerful groups. The coalitional aspects of policymaking can be observed in Table 9, which describes competition among alternative policies and how coalition building eventually determines public policy.

From Table 9 one can observe the policy preferences of three congressional representatives: one from a rural farm district, one from an urban area with high crime and high drug abuse, and one from a poor district of Appalachia, which is neither a major farm nor a major crime area. Policy preferences were recorded in Table 9 for each of the three districts on an ordinal scale with one (1.00) representing the highest policy priority and three (3.00) representing the policy priority with the lowest preference. For the sake of simplicity, only three policy choices were considered in Table 9. Each of these three alternative policies (expand farm subsidies, create a food stamp program, and expand crime and drug programs) had the same $5 billion price tag, and it was assumed that only one of the three programs would be passed. Given another

Table 9
Policy Competition and Coalition Building

Policies	Decision Makers			
	Farm	Urban	Poverty	Sum of Ordinal
	District	District	District	Preferences
Expand Farm Subsidies ($5 billion)	1.0	3.0	2.5	6.5
Create a New Food Stamp Program ($5 billion)	2.0	2.0	1.0	5.0
Expand Crime and Drug Programs ($5 billion)	3.0	1.0	2.5	6.5

assumption, that all representatives vote their self-interest, the program with the most widespread political appeal (the food stamp program) is predicted to be passed.

The food stamp program generated the highest level of political support because it received some support from both the farm and urban districts as well as primary support from the generic poverty district. Assuming low numbers of drug addicts in the rural district, a drug program would hold little value. Similarly, assuming low numbers of farmers in the urban district, a farm subsidy program would have a low priority. A food stamp program, however, would provide some benefits to both farmers (in terms of additional farm sales) and to the urban poor, who could qualify for nutritional benefits. For this reason, the food stamp program was ranked as a second-order priority (2.00) in both the rural and urban districts and was ranked as the first-order priority (1.00) in the generic poverty district. The ultimate result was a higher aggregate priority score (5.00) for the food stamp program and lower-priority scores (6.5) for both the farm subsidy and drug programs. Because the food stamp program was more acceptable to a larger number of groups, it received the largest level of support. Because of its vote-attracting appeal, the political model of budgeting predicts that this policy would be adopted.

The foregoing scenario is analogous to policymaking in the U.S. Congress, where "vote swapping" is a fact of life. Of course, in Congress there are more than three representatives and more than three policy areas. Anthony Downs uses this concept of vote trading and coalition building to create a more sophisticated model. In his model, public policies were seen to be the result of the process of vote maximization. Priority is perceived to be given to projects that gain the most votes and lose the fewest votes. Public programs are therefore funded until the vote gain of the last dollar spent equals the vote loss of the last dollar financed.[25] Downs replaced the economic concept of funding policies that maximize social welfare with the political concept of approving policies that maximize votes. Utilizing the Downsian vote maximization model, one can see why politically appealing projects, such as dams and water projects, receive support in legislatures irrespective of their benefit to society as a whole. Passage of programs amenable to coalition building, such as the food stamp program, are also readily explained by the vote maximization model developed by Downs.

The vote maximization model represents only one perspective of the political component of policymaking. As previously stated, ideology plays a role in the development of specific mind sets and consequently in the development of values that shape resource allocations. In the United States, values that can be placed on a liberal-conservative continuum are said to dominate. These contrasting values affect positions on fundamental issues such as the role of government in both the affairs of individuals and the economy as a whole. Groups sympathetic to one philosophy or another help to shape public opinion, which in turn influences policy priorities. In order to gain insight into how these ideological values influence policy, economic perspectives of both liberals and conservatives in the United States are discussed. It is believed that economic perspectives of liberals and conservatives will shape policy postures and will ultimately help to determine resource allocations.

LIBERAL ECONOMIC PERSPECTIVE

There remains a great deal of confusion surrounding the term "liberalism." C. B. MacPherson contended that liberalism meant so many things to so many people that it was easily misunderstood.[26] Confusion exists because its meaning has changed over time. An example of this confusion is witnessed in the differentiation between "classical liberalism" and liberalism today.

Classical liberalism is perhaps best illustrated in the works of Adam Smith, who extolled the free market and criticized the mercantilist philosophies of sovereigns of his day. An alternative to the classical economic perspective was postulated by John Maynard Keynes in his book *General Theory of Employment, Interest, and Money*. Keynes's view revolutionized economic thought of his day. It rested upon the contention that a monetary system could be managed to promote economic stability and mitigate the harmful effects of depression. According to Keynes, public policies could "fine tune" the economy in order to stabilize economic fluctuations. Keynesian theory hypothesized that the amount of investment depended upon the degree of new investment, which in turn was dependent upon the rate of interest. If at any time the rate of interest could be lowered, and if there were no changes in business expectations of profit, the amount of new investment would increase, stimulating the economy.[27] In order to increase economic activity and reduce unemployment, Keynes recommended increasing the supply of money and lowering interest rates. As interest rates fell, businesses would be more willing to borrow and greater economic growth would follow.

Keynesian economics is valued for its promise of stability and growth. Both of these outcomes are perceived to be the result of government control of interest rates and the money supply. Government could increase economic activity by the use of fiscal policy (lowering taxes and increasing public sector spending) or monetary policy (expand the supply of economic resources available to the private sector by actions of the Federal Reserve System). Fiscal and monetary policy were considered companion tools of the public sector in efforts to control the economy. Keynes explained that high unemployment could be combatted through increased government spending. He believed that unemployment would fall when government spending rose because consumers would have more dollars to purchase goods and services, which in turn would lead to higher levels of production. Monetary policy was another tool to stimulate the economy by increasing the availability of money and reducing the cost of borrowing. Declines in the rate of interest would encourage corporations to borrow funds to create new facilities, and in turn create new jobs.[28]

Keynesian philosophy was noted for its success in reorienting economic thought away from laissez-faire economics or nonintervention toward the acceptance of government activity in the marketplace. Keynes developed a system whereby the overall level of economic activity had to be managed to serve all citizens, yet the economy would still be free to respond to decisions of individual producers and consumers.[29] Hope was offered that government could mitigate the severe economic crisis of the Great Depression. According to Paul Samuelson, Keynes's classic 1936 text, *The General Theory of Employment, Interest, and Money,* created the greatest stir in economic thinking of the century.[30]

CONSERVATIVE ECONOMIC PERSPECTIVE

Conservatives differ from liberals in the United States in regard to fundamental economic perspectives. Two characteristics of conservatives are said to be clinging to the notions of laissez-faire economic principles and clinging to the virtues of economic individualism. Consistent with the values of individualism and laissez-faire economics are the principles of a noninterventionist state with low levels of taxation. It is believed that low tax levels would provide incentives for risk taking and profit maximization. These principles are inherent in what has come to be known as "supply-side economics."

The supply-side message was heavily supported by the Reagan administration. Reagan's fealty with this philosophy was enunciated in his budget message of January 1981. According to this doctrine, the federal budget was to be balanced via a policy of substantial tax reduction. It was believed that lower tax burdens would stimulate growth in such a manner that the revenue lost from the tax cut would be recouped through increases in the size of the total economic pie.[31] The theory of supply-side economics (tax cuts leading to economic growth) also provided the stimulus for the passage of the Economic Recovery Tax Act of 1981. This act, better known by the names of its key supporters, Jack Kemp and William Roth, reduced personal income taxes by 25 percent over a thirty-three-month period. It anticipated that taxpayers would save much of the money that they received through lower taxes and that the increased savings would lead to increased investment and growth. The view of the Reagan administration was that once the deadening weight of government was reduced, the private sector would be invigorated and growth of the economy would ensue.[32]

Advocates of supply-side economics maintained that incentives such as higher profits must be provided. In the absence of such incentives, producers are perceived to eschew risks and innovation. They are more likely to place their money in nonproductive tax shelters such as art work or race horses. In this scenario, producers would take greater risks if they were allowed to retain a greater proportion of their profits. The Laffer curve, explaining the basic concept behind supply-side economics, is described in Figure 6.1.

According to economist Arthur Laffer, all production ceases in the money economy when the tax rate is 100 percent. This is perfectly logical: if all the fruits of one's economic labor were confiscated, there would be absolutely no incentive to work and production might conceivably approach zero in the taxable economy. Conversely, if one kept the entire value of one's production, the government's share would again approach zero. Within these two extremes, the governing body has a wide degree of discretion in regard to setting levels of taxation. According to the theory represented in the Laffer curve, the public sector can increase its revenues by raising taxes, but a point is reached when raising taxes will not produce increased revenue; on the contrary, increased taxation will continuously decrease the level of public revenue until it approaches zero. This is said to occur because at higher levels of taxation people will move into the barter economy, not work as diligently, or not work at all. This in turn will reduce the aggregate level of economic activity. A lower tax rate, on the other hand, will produce more revenue because the growth of the economy is believed to more than make up for the lower levels of taxes.

The upper region of the Laffer curve is termed the "prohibitive" range because tax increases in this range will result in both decreased private sector output and decreased public sector revenues. Public sector revenues will be maximized at point Z. This point is not a tax rate of 50 percent but represents the point at which the electorate is willing to be taxed without a corresponding decrease in effort. At points V and X, the public will increase output if taxes are lowered; this will in turn increase aggregate public revenue—that is, the increase in the total economic activity will more than make up for the lower marginal tax rate.

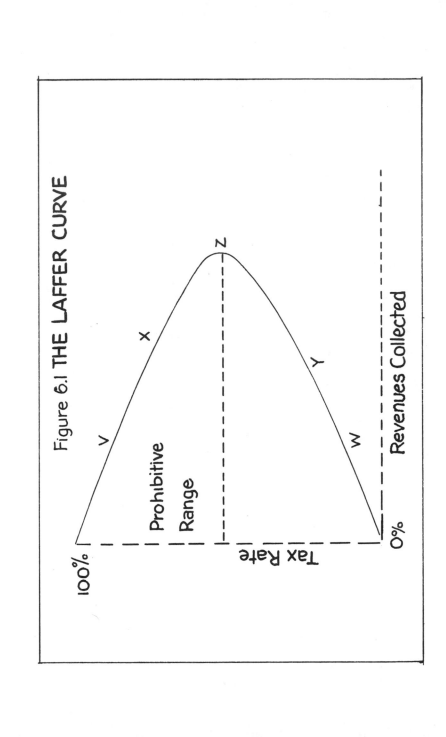

Figure 6.1 THE LAFFER CURVE

Point Z on the Laffer curve is determined by the attitudes of the people. This point is not fixed but is determined by the external environment and the public's willingness or unwillingness to release income to a collective body. It was noted that at the siege of Leningrad in World War II, the people willingly produced for over two and a half years at tax rates approaching 100 percent.[33] This corresponds to point Z on the Laffer curve but represents an extreme distention of the curve as a result of the perceived consequences of refusing to contribute to the war effort.

George Gilder further described how tax rates affect total output. Gilder provided a justification for the Laffer curve with his assertion that high taxes produce an increase in the value of nonproductive assets and a decline in the value of productive assets. Taxes are said to distort the free competitive market and produce "sumps" of wealth or sink holes of purchasing power that shift money to nonproductive tax shelters. Demand for these nonproductive tax shelters results in lower levels of productive investment, which in turn depresses growth of the economy. According to Gilder, economies grow "in response to the enterprise of men willing to take risks to transform ideas into monopolies, and monopolies into industries."[34]

Government is viewed by Gilder as more likely to produce proliferating bureaucracies than innovation and growth. Growth is seen to occur when individuals are given the opportunity to keep more of what they create (i.e., when taxes are lower). As decreed in the supply-side doctrine, supply, not demand, is perceived to be the real engine of economic growth:

Aggregate demand is an effect of production, not of government policy. The only way tax policy can reliably influence real incomes is by changing the incentives of suppliers. By altering the pattern of rewards to favor work over leisure, investment over consumption, the sources of production over the sumps of wealth, taxable over nontaxable activity, government can directly and powerfully foster the expansion of real demand and income. This is the supply side mandate.[35]

The supply-side perspective of low taxes relates to the classical liberal (contemporary conservative) perspective of limited government intervention in the free marketplace and directly contradicts the Keynesian perspective of positive government influence. Milton Friedman, perhaps the best-known advocate of the free market today, declared that whenever the state undertakes to control the economic activities of citizens, the amount of freedom and the standard of living of those citizens will decline. In contrast, Friedman claimed that whenever there exists a large element of individual freedom, some measure of progress in the material comforts will be found at the disposal of ordinary citizens, and widespread hope of further progress in the future will exist. These conditions are said to exist in spite of the view of intellectuals that free enterprise capitalism and a free market are devices for exploiting the masses while central economic planning is the wave of the future that will set their countries on the road to rapid economic progress.[36]

Friedman claimed that the superiority of free market capitalism can be observed through contrasting the prosperity of free market countries with that of countries operating under controlled economies. The most obvious example is said to be the contrast between East and West Germany, where "people of the same blood, the same civilization, the same level of technical knowledge inhabit the two parts." According to Friedman, in East Berlin "the streets appear empty: the city gray and pallid; the store windows, dull; the buildings grimy," whereas in the western sector of the city, "the brightly lit streets and stores are filled with cheerful, bustling people" buying "newspapers and magazines expressing every variety of opinion."[37]

The perspectives of Friedman, Gilder, and Laffer prioritize values such as individualism, innovation, creativity, and individual incentive. Fundamental differences exist between these perspectives and those of Keynesian economists. The conservative ideal advocates limited government intervention and the desire for the "genius" of the free market to work its magic. The liberal ideal tends to reject the view that the free market, left to itself, will provide the greatest good for the greatest number. Abuses of private power are seen as inevitable; therefore, government has a responsibility to control the negative externalities resulting from unfettered competition.

There is much evidence to support the notion that political rather than economic explanations explain public policy-making. Values are imbedded in our fundamental political positions. Individuals and groups are shaped by values, and values guide behavior. Due to the effects of these values on policy, political ideologies probably influence policy positions to a far greater extent than is readily admitted.

Ideals inherent in ideologies such as socialism, capitalism, fascism, and nationalism cannot help but influence political discussion today. Nationalist sentiment is found in positions prioritizing patriotism, the threats to the United States from foreign countries, and increased defense expenditures. Fascist strains may be seen in positions that support the increase of centralized power as well as in policies advocating increased government intrusion into the marketplace through arrangements among business, labor, and government. Socialist thought is observed in policy positions that prioritize spending for programs advocating greater social equity. Capitalist core values are witnessed in programs that prioritize lower taxes and less government intervention.

Knowledge of political ideologies is essential for policy analysts today. This knowledge should be used to decouple objective policy analysis from ideology. Only if ideological thinking can be identified and controlled will greater objectivity begin to play a larger role in policymaking. With more objective analysis of public policy, the public may one day gain a better understanding of policy impacts. The public will be better able to make intelligent judgments about public policies and will be better served through a more objective understanding of the underpinnings of policy positions. The impact of ideology on public policy is apparent from a review of the budget experiences of the Reagan administration.

BUDGETING IN THE REAGAN ADMINISTRATION

Budgeting policy under the Reagan administration, according to some sources, has been unduly politicized. In the sense that he had a very clear idea about policy priorities and about how the world works, Reagan could be considered highly ideological. This characterization implies that fixed conceptions of the world had been developed on the basis of less than a totally objective conception of reality. Individualistic experiences of Reagan rather than objective analysis may have contributed to the development of policy. This may be especially true in regard to attitudes toward taxation. Perhaps policy evaluation today is so unreliable that intuitive beliefs on the basis of personal experience are superior to the so-called objective tests. This may be true in individualized instances but is a very dangerous strategy to employ across the board.

Instead of intuitive policymaking based upon personal experiences, gut feelings, or political perspectives, greater rationality should enhance analysis of policy choices and should be built into the structure of public policymaking. This may not occur, however, until the field of policy analysis gains greater credibility and respectability. In an age when one can find "experts" to testify on behalf of almost any policy position, it is not surprising that decision makers sometimes rely upon intuition when formulating policy. The sentiment that one can hire statisticians to argue any position further undermines the view that rational analysis of public policies is both desirable and attainable.

Many analysts claim that the Reagan administration harnessed ideological zeal in order to make sweeping changes in American public policy. From the perspective of the committed activist, the changes were unquestionably of great benefit to the nation. From the perspective of the neutral policy analyst, however, more careful deliberation should have occurred prior to inauguration of sweeping programs.

Major budgetary changes did occur in the Reagan administration. Reagan's budget legislation has been considered by some to be revolutionary because of the size and scope of the changes.[38] Gregory Mills noted that in the period preceding the Reagan administration, the federal tax burden increased from 18.5 percent of gross national product in 1959 to 20.8 percent in 1979. Mills also found that between 1960 and 1980, for a family of four with a median income, federal income taxes and social security payroll taxes increased as a percentage of income from 10.1 to 17.5 percent. Both trends were reversed in the Reagan administration. The across-the-board tax cuts introduced in 1981 were said to be the cornerstone of the Reagan economic program.[39]

Perhaps the most significant of all the budgetary changes experienced under Reagan was the reversal of the steady growth in nondefense expenditures. In 1961, nondefense spending constituted 8.1 percent of gross national product; by 1981 it had almost doubled, to 15.7 percent of GNP, however, by 1984 it had been trimmed to 14.1 percent. Defense spending in the Reagan administration increased significantly. This increase, the decline in nondefense spending, and the cuts in taxes were all consistent with the conservative political ideology espoused by Reagan in the 1980 and 1984 presidential campaigns.

All budget outcomes did not correspond to outcomes that could be predicted solely from an understanding of ideology. The Reagan administration was unable to reduce total government spending and failed miserably in its attempts to balance the budget. Revenues fell with the tax cuts but total federal spending rose, and the increase in spending was funded by borrowing. This eliminated the possibility of balancing the budget in the Reagan era.

Allen Schick, noted budget analyst, provided some explanation for the growth of expenditures during the conservative Reagan administration. According to Schick, federal spending continued to rise under Reagan "because of higher interest payments (due to big deficits and high interest rates), increased defense spending, and the programmed rise in entitlement programs."[40]

Entitlement programs accounted for more than $400 billion in expenditures in 1985. These programs were largely uncontrollable; amounts expended were dependent upon factors such as the number of persons eligible to receive payments for specific programs. Most entitlement programs, such as Social Security, were also indexed to a price adjuster; as a result, expenditures automatically rose during periods of inflation. Entitlements could not easily be reduced because they represented legal rights to payments from the federal treasury. The Reagan administration did try to limit entitlement payments through changes in eligibility requirements. All in all, however, it was unsuccessful in capping the bulk of the payments. Social Security (the largest of the entitlement programs) has grown significantly over the years. In 1954, Social Security and other social insurance programs cost about $25 billion (in 1986 dollars), or 1.5 percent of GNP. By 1980, these programs cost $230 billion (in 1986 dollars), or 6.5 percent of GNP. Social Security spending amounted to $288 billion in 1986.[41]

A second factor explaining the growth of expenditures during the conservative Reagan administration was the high interest payments brought about by the large deficits. Interest payments on the public debt accounted for $179 billion in 1985, more than 10 percent of total federal expenditures.[42] The third large contributor to expenditure growth was defense spending. National defense as a category of spending grew to approximately $290 billion in 1987, up sharply from $142 billion in 1980.[43]

How ideology contributed to a policy of deficits is explained by the first head of the Office of Management and

Budgets in the Reagan administration, David Stockman. Stockman described how political ideology blocked more objective assessments of policy options:

We had ended up with a high growth–low inflation consensus forecast on the basis of pure doctrine. Nobody was running the economic forecasts through the OMB budget models to see what kind of deficit you got. . . . A huge irony was thus in the making. Had the ideologues stuck with their purist forecasts, the Reagan Revolution would not have been launched on February 18–and perhaps never. The staggering magnitude of domestic spending cuts necessary to balance the budget would have caused the White House politicians to lurch out of their slumber.[44]

Stockman's account of his White House days paints a picture of bureaucrats who willingly sacrificed rational analysis in an effort to secure ideological goals. These goals were lower taxes, lower domestic spending, and higher defense spending. It appears that a rational choice was not made by the top managers (the president and Congress) to accept deficits as the price for other budget priorities. Objective budgetary analysis seems to have been discarded because the full implications of the tax decrease and miltary build up were never fully spelled out. What was presented was the view that the Reagon program could be implemented without massive deficits. Stockman's manipulation of the books made a rational choice of policy trade-offs impossible. He stated that to hide future deficits, he invented the "magic asterisk." This magic asterisk would "cost negative $30 billion, $40 billion, whatever it took to get a balanced budget in 1984."[45] Stockman called his asterisk a "marvelous creation," yet it prevented higher-level policymakers from making hard choices based upon the best available data. Ideological fervor was employed to prevent the fullest exercise of rationality by the relevant decision makers. By manipulation of the data, both rationality and democratic principles were subverted.

The presence or absence of support for Reagan's landmark budget legislation was predictable based upon an understanding of prevailing ideologies. Tip O'Neill, speaker of the House of Representatives, stated in 1981 that the Reagan budget would "change the nation back to before the 1930's."[46] He further contended that Reagan's spending plan represented "a trap, not a safety net," that Reagan would "meat-ax the programs that made America great," and that Reagan's budget ideas would "close the door on America."[47] In contrast to O'Neill's perspective, the minority leader of the House of Representatives, Robert Michel, argued that Reagan's budget represented a "giant leap for the country."[48] Reagan maintained that he was simply carrying out the will of the people with his programs, and that his plan was the "only answer we have left" to cure the ills of the economy.[49]

It seems clear that both ideology and party allegiance influenced individual perspectives in regard to public policy. The rhetoric surrounding Reagan's budget and tax plans indicates that in a democracy it is possible for ideology to replace neutral analysis of policy options. This is just and proper from the perspective of the truly committed ideologues, yet the consequences of ideologically biased public policy may be severe. The impacts of such policy may be enormous and unfortunately not realized until well into the future. Inevitably, future generations will either benefit or suffer from the actions of their predecessors. It is encumbent upon the current generation to prevent the transfer of great burdens into the future. Greater levels of rationality and objectivity in the public policy process will work toward the accomplishment of this goal.

NOTES

1. Anthony Downs, *An Economic Theory of Democracy* (New York: Harper & Row, 1957).

2. James Buchanan, "The Pure Theory of Government Finance: A Suggested Approach," *Journal of Political Economy* 57 (December 1949): 496–505.

3. Downs, *An Economic Theory of Democracy*, p. 52.

4. Ibid., p. 70.

5. William Niskanen, Jr., *Bureaucracy and Representative Government* (Chicago: Aldine, 1971), p. 38.

6. A. C. Pigou, *A Study in Public Finance* (London: Macmillan, 1928), p. 50.

7. V. O. Key, Jr., "The Lack of a Budgetary Theory," *American Political Science Review* 34 (December 1940): 1137-44.

8. Quoted in Aaron Wildavsky, "Rescuing Policy Analysis from PPBS," *Public Administration Review* 29 (March/April 1969): 189-202.

9. Verne Lewis, "Toward a Theory of Budgeting," *Public Administration Review* 12, no. 1 (Winter 1952): 42-54.

10. Ibid.

11. Peter Pyhrr, "The Zero-Base Approach to Government Budgeting," *Public Administration Review* 37 (January-February 1977): 1-8.

12. Aaron Wildavsky, *The Politics of the Budgetary Process* (Boston: Little, Brown, 1984), pp. 200-201.

13. Henry Tosi and Stephen Carroll, "Management by Objectives," in *A New World: Readings on Modern Public Personnel Management*, ed. Jay Shafritz (Chicago: International Personnel Management Association, 1975), pp. 179-83.

14. Jong S. Jun, "Management by Objectives in the Public Sector," *Public Administration Review* 36, no. 1 (January-February 1976): 3.

15. Wildavsky, *The Politics of the Budgetary Process*, p. 196.

16. David Braybrook and Charles Lindblom, *A Strategy of Decision* (New York: Free Press, 1970), pp. 48-53.

17. Ludwig von Mises, *Bureaucracy* (New Haven, Conn.: Yale University Press, 1944), p. 47.

18. Charles Tiebout, "A Pure Theory of Local Expenditures," *Journal of Political Economy* 64 (October 1956): 416-24.

19. Paul Samuelson, "The Pure Theory of Public Expenditures," *Review of Economics and Statistics* 36 (November 1954): 387-89; Richard Musgrave, "The Voluntary Exchange Theory of Public Economy," *Quarterly Journal of Economics* 53 (February 1939): 213-17.

20. Carol Weiss, "The Many Meanings of Research Utilization," in *Program Evaluation: Patterns and Directions*, ed. E. Chelimsky (Washington, D.C.: American Society for Public Administration, 1985), p. 207.

21. Wildavsky, *The Politics of the Budgetary Process*, p. 176.

22. Aaron Wildavsky, "Political Implications of Budgetary Reform," *Public Administration Review* 21 (Autumn 1961): 183-90.

23. David Truman, *The Governmental Process* (New York: Alfred Knopf, 1951).

24. Wildavsky, *The Politics of the Budgetary Process*, p. 5.

25. Downs, *An Economic Theory of Democracy*, p. 52.

26. C. B. MacPherson, "The False Roots of Western Democracy," in *From Contract to Community*, ed. Fred R. Dallmayr (New York: Marcel Dekker, 1978), p. 17.

27. Daniel Fusfeld, *The Age of the Economist* (Glenview, Ill.: Scott, Foresman, 1982), p. 102.

29. Robert Lee, Jr., and Ronald Johnson, *Public Budgeting Systems* (Baltimore: University Park Press, 1983), p. 347.

29. Fusfeld, *The Age of the Economist*, p. 105.

30. Paul Samuelson, *Economics An Introductory Analysis* (New York: McGraw-Hill, 1964), p. 205.

31. Richard Musgrave and Peggy Musgrave, *Public Finance in Theory and Practice* (New York: McGraw-Hill, 1984), p. 648.

32. Lee and Johnson, *Public Budgeting Systems*, p. 347.

33. Jude Wanniski, *The Way the World Works* (New York: Simon and Schuster, 1978), p. 98.

34. George Gilder, *Wealth and Poverty* (New York: Basic Books, 1981), p. 39.

35. Ibid., p. 46.

36. Milton Friedman and Rose Friedman, *Free to Choose* (New York: Avon, 1979), p. 46.

37. Ibid., p. 47.

38. Robert W. Hartman, "Congress and Budget-Making," in *New Directions in Public Administration*, ed. B. Bozeman and J. Straussman (Belmont, Calif.: Brooks/Cole, 1984), p. 129.

39. Gregory B. Mills, "The Budget: A Failure of Discipline," in *The Reagan Record*, ed. John Palmer and Isabel Sawhill (Cambridge, Mass.: Ballinger, 1984), pp. 110-11.

40. Allen Schick, "Incremental Budgeting in a Decremental Age," in *Current Issues in Public Administration*, ed. Frederick Lane (New York: St. Martin's Press, 1986), p. 291.

41. David Stockman, *The Triumph of Politics* (New York: Harper & Row, 1986), pp. 401-9.

42. *Congressional Quarterly* 44, no. 6 (8 February 1986): 257.

43. *New York Times*, 16 October 1986.

44. Stockman, *The Triumph of Politics*, p. 94.

45. Ibid., p. 124.

46. Peter Goldman et al., "The Second Hundred Days," *Newsweek*, 11 May 1981, p. 24.

47. Peter Goldman et al., "The Reagan Steamroller," *Newsweek*, 18 May 1981, pp. 38-40.

48. Ed Magnusus, "Reagan's Big Win," *Time*, 18 May 1981, pp. 14-16.

49. Goldman et al., "The Second Hundred Days," p. 24.

7

Conclusions

Ideology undoubtedly affects budgets and public policy-making in general. A fundamental question to be asked, therefore, is whether this influence is positive or negative. In regard to its implications toward democratic theory, ideological policy can be positively construed because in this scenario, free people choose candidates of identifiable beliefs, and those candidates implement policies that reflect the popular will. Public accountability is attained in this process, and power ultimately can be traced to the populace. On the other hand, ideological policymaking can be perceived as negative. The negative aspects of ideological policymaking arise when poor public policy is developed as a result of blind adherence to doctrine. Preconceived perspectives and the development of narrow mind sets may result in poor policy because they hinder objective assessments of policy success or failure. Poor policy and suboptimum use of resources may result. An infusion of greater rationality in the policymaking process, it is hoped, will result in a more effective and efficient policy.

In the extreme case, ideological budgeting reflects blatant irrationality justified on the basis of emotion and passion. It is therefore a threat to values of neutral competence and values of administration developed long ago. Woodrow Wilson, back in 1887, recognized the presence of political threats to efficient public service and advocated that the field of administration be removed from the sphere of politics. Wilson promoted this "dichotomy" between politics and administration in order to create professional public servants who would be unaffected by the political pressures and corruption that surrounded the political domain. Politics in Wilson's era was associated with corrupt "machines" and inefficiency in contrast to the image of "good government" associated with professional administrators.[1]

Wilson's ideas were embraced by reformers of the early 1900s who desired efficiency and honesty in government. The separation of politics from administration became known as the "politics-administration" dichotomy and was consistent with the perspective that there was no Democratic or Republican way to perform specific governmental functions. Government was perceived as a bundle of functional responsibilities to be managed efficiently, rather than a profession by which to reap personal rewards. The value of neutral competence was elevated and was perceived as essential for the implementation of public policy. This perspective sharply contrasted with the ethic of political patronage that dominated public life in Wilson's era.

The ideal of neutral competence was buttressed by the perception that value-free social science can become a reality. Max Weber believed that social science researchers could (and should) separate empirical facts from value-laden assessments. Weber stated that whenever the scientist introduced value judgments into analysis, full understanding ceased. Science, according to Weber, would not involve "prophets dispensing sacred values" but would be organized along special disciplines in the service of knowledge.[2]

Weber contended that policies of government could be objectively formulated and evaluated. Once a goal had been established, policy could be created that was untainted by ideological rhetoric or other confounding influences. The real effect of public policy on the environment and the success of the policy in terms of goal fulfillment could then be rationally tested.

Neutrality and intersubjectivity in the evaluation of public policies are not realities today because of the many abuses of policy analysis. Commonly cited policy abuses include the eyewash (looking only at the good aspects of programs), the whitewash (completely cover up program failure), the submarine (destroy a program regardless of its worth), postponement (delay necessary action), and substitution (shift attention to a less relevant but defensible aspect of a program). Abuses such as these must be eliminated if social scientists are to obtain greater respect and credibility.[3]

An example of how values can result in the implementation of biased policy is provided next. Table 10 illustrates how slanted evaluations of public policies can lead to poor policy decisions. The broad policy goal that is examined here is "greater safety," which can be operationalized through measures such as growth in the rate of violent crime. Even with objective measures such as crime rates as a guide, the evaluation of policies aimed at achieving the broad policy goal may be biased. Table 10 describes how biased evaluations may reinforce poor policy. In the first case of Table 10, there is virtually no policy effect. An ideologically biased evaluation, however, can lead to reinforcement of this policy. The biased evaluation may falsely give the impression that the policy is effective. In the second case, sound policy is rejected

Table 10
Reinforcement of Poor Policy

Broad Policy	Policy Effect	Evaluation
1. Greater Safety	No Impact	Biased (Reinforced)
2. Greater Safety	Positive Impact	Biased (Rejected)

Table 11
Rejection of Poor Policy

Broad Policy	Policy Effect	Evaluation
1. Greater Safety	No Impact	Unbiased (Rejected)
2. Greater Safety	Positive Impact	Unbiased (Reinforced)

because biased evaluations produced an incorrect assessment of the true policy impact. These are common problems that confront public officials. This problem can be addressed only when more methodological rigor is attained. Application of good research designs utilizing control groups will be a positive step in improving our understanding of the true effects of public policy.

In Table 11 the improper decision making and interpretation of policy found in Table 10 is avoided; evaluations in this scenario are assumed to be both valid and reliable. The broad policy goal of greater safety is the same as found in Table 10. However, in this instance the inferior policy is rejected and the superior policy is reinforced. Rationality is achieved because the biases of ideological influences are eliminated. Implementation of objective evaluations (such as assumed in Table 11) is a goal that should be pursued but one that is not easily achieved.

Ideologies can bias evaluations and can therefore influence strategies of dealing with broad societal problems. Liberals and conservatives differ in regard to their attitudes toward broad societal problems. Attitudes differ in regard to the question of how to deal with specific problems. Differences in connection with policies related to poverty and education are apparent. The conservative approach to poverty maintains that welfare should be strictly limited to those who cannot work in the regular job market. "Workfare" is advocated in order to work off part of the welfare benefits at public jobs paying minimum wage or very close to the minimum wage.

Conservatives are also skeptical about the benefits of government intervention in the economy and believe that the free market should be left alone to deal with the problems of poverty and unemployment that exist in our society.

The liberal approach to the issue of welfare differs significantly from the approach described earlier. The liberal approach tends to advocate more intervention by the federal government. Setting federal standards for welfare benefits and placing welfare fully under federal control are favored policy positions. Some liberals also advocate full employment guaranteed by the government and have much less faith in the free marketplace.

Education policy provides the second specific example of the different perspectives to policy problems held by liberals and conservatives. The liberal point of view reflects the democratic ideal that equality must be balanced with liberty and efficiency. According to Diane Ravitch, education in a liberal society must hold in balance two ideals that coexist in tension: equality and excellence.[4] Given that the free market is viewed as incapable of achieving such a balance, education must be the responsibility of the government. Liberals believe that the government must construct a public school system that rewards ability without promoting elitism. To accomplish this end, action is perceived to be necessary on three fronts: greater equality in school financing, greater equality in racial integration, and special emphasis on helping educationally deprived groups.

The conservative approach to education policy focuses on the efficiency and productivity of school systems. Conservatives focus on cost and the quality of education. Blame for a poor educational system is placed on the government. The perceived solution to present problems of education is to break government's control of schools through strategies such as tuition tax credits, public aid to private schools, increased public school tuition, and voucher plans. Competency tests for both students and teachers are viewed as a method for enforcing higher standards.[5] Again, it is clear that although liberals and conservatives both want "better" education for the nation's children, the perceived methods to attain that goal differ considerably.

A well-know liberal columnist stated that ideology was king in Washington with devastating results across the range of public policies. The columnist claimed that the United States faced the disease AIDS, which might be the greatest menace to public health in the nation's history. Urgent recommendations for government action were needed, yet a commission on AIDS was said to be "shattered by ideology." Henry Waxman, congressional representative from California, further stated that many members of the commission "were appointed either because they knew nothing about AIDS or had already made up their minds to go along with a right-wing agenda rather than a public health agenda in dealing with disease."[6]

Ideology has exerted a greater influence on the national bureaucracy in recent years. In the last 20 years, Presidents Nixon, Carter, and Reagan have all perceived the permanent bureaucracy to be ideologically different from their views and have tried to appoint individuals to the bureaucracy who were more in line with their own ideological thinking. Patricia Ingraham claimed that large numbers of political appointees with notably short tenure in public life had recently invaded the bureaucracy. She noted that these political appointees often lacked preparation for their jobs, and therefore a large proportion of their time was spent "learning the ropes." Ingraham concluded that the impact of these political appoint-ments was negative in terms of the quality of public manage-ment. By ignoring career experts, critical resources were squandered. The short-term political perspective of appointees also hindered effectiveness since they did not adequately con-sider long-term policy impacts.[7]

James Pfiffner also argued that increased politicization was counterproductive to effective government. He stated that "the capacity of the White House is being undermined by the present trend toward increasing numbers of political appointees. Reversing this direction would increase the capacity of the government to function efficiently and effectively without sacrificing political accountability or responsiveness."[8] He further claimed that the bureaucratic machine of the nation must be in place and ready to respond to new directives. This capacity would be greatly impaired if "bureaucracy is completely decapitated with each change in administration."[9]

These concerns about the state of the bureaucracy were echoed by the former chairman of the Federal Reserve Board, Paul Volcker. Volcker, speaking as the chair of the National Commission on Public Service, remarked that "somebody has to defend the nation, somebody has to make the rules and enforce them, somebody has to build the roads, and somebody even has to control the money supply. And I think people think that they're entitled to see those jobs done with a little continuity and professionalism."[10] Volcker expressed concern that the reservoir of expertise and professionalism in the ranks of the government had dropped and that the best of the country's young graduates had gravitated to Wall Street instead of Washington. Furthermore, if they did end up in Washington, Volcker stated it would be to run a lobby or represent a client, not to represent the public.

Liberals and conservatives often cannot agree on means to reach common ends, so they often speak past one another with little gained from the experience. Policy evaluation has the potential to mediate agreements between people of differing perspectives. Given the state of the art of policy analysis today, however, there is little guarantee that greater rationality can be achieved in the evaluation of policies. Public policies therefore must be developed as a result of electoral victory or defeat of groups adhering to different ideological positions. Democratic theorists would find value in this process because the people would ultimately have input into the system.

Problems with this approach exist, however. Voters may be misled or influenced by political campaigns that appear to support their interests but in reality do much to harm them. Another problem is that politicians may win elections on the basis of emotional slogans that only tangentially relate to public policy issues. Once in power, elected leaders may deal with specific problems in a manner that was not predictable based on the electoral campaign.

It is conceivable that more openmindedness and rational testing of various policy options could narrow the gap between liberal and conservative policy postures. Rationality and truly objective evaluation research could conceivably produce policies that would be more successful in achieving the goals of our society. Broad goals such as better security, health, education, and economic opportunities are generally accepted. The perceived means to achieve those ends, however, differ because of different philosophical perspectives held by leaders.

The validity of ideological assumptions and their usefulness in achieving desired ends is a question that must be addressed when trying to formulate public policies. Which ideological assumptions are more useful in achieving the desired end should be considered more of an empirical question than one of political conflict. Success of specific policies in achieving desired ends could be empirically explored if policy evaluations were neutral and attained an acceptable degree of rigor. The science of policy analysis should be further developed in order to investigate the utility of various approaches in achieving agreed-upon goals.

This book has addressed the issue of how ideology directly or indirectly shapes our public policies. In 1887, Woodrow Wilson presented the vision that administration in the public sector can be rational, neutral, and removed from political influences. This ideal vision is yet to be realized but has served as a model for advocates of a professionalized, incorruptible public sector. Wilson's vision should not be undermined today.

As with his vision of the League of Nations, perhaps he was correct but his ideas not yet politically feasible. If we are to achieve a more efficient and effective government, we must seriously investigate inherent biases that exist in our thinking. and work to eliminate them. Through the elimination of philosophical biases we should be able to produce sounder and more effective public policy.

The benefits of rational rather than ideological policy seem to be intuitively obvious. The triumph of ideological over rational policy presents administrators with a real dilemma. Ideology must be separated from administration. The need for a new dichotomy (an "ideology-administration" dichotomy) should be recognized. Blind adherence to ideology is as corrupting today as machine patronage was to Woodrow Wilson in 1887. Both ideology- and reward-based spoils represent threats to the ethic of neutral competence.

Some theorists may advocate policy developed by political appointees who fervently believe in their own set of policy prescriptions. Others believe that policy should be developed by neutral administrators trained in specific career fields. A more balanced view is that both are essential—the political zealots and the career bureaucrats. The zealots provide enthusiasm while the career officials provide continuity and balance. It is essential that balance be maintained and that the fulcrum of policy does not shift too far in favor of political zealots who desire to implement policy that may be hopelessly flawed. If separation of administration from ideology is attained through the "ideology-administration" dichotomy discussed above, bureaucrats will be insulated from ideological zealots who are committed to a certain normative vision. This dichotomy bears some similarity to Wilson's vision but is different in that civil servants will be protected from ideological zealots rather than from incompetent and dishonest patronage appointees who have been rewarded for their loyalty to a political party.

Ideological policies may be formed when zealots such as

Lt. Colonel Oliver North fervently believe in the righteousness of their cause. We should not, however, mistake fervor for wisdom. There is no guarantee that "gut" feelings of political appointees or even of individual politicians will produce policies superior to those developed by neutral bureaucrats. It is reasonable to believe that policies developed as a result of careful study of prior experiences would be wiser and safer than policies developed as a result of philosophy and intuition. A truly professional and respected public service will be most beneficial to the nation in the long term.

The task of developing greater rationality in the formulation of public policy faces enormous problems. However, if analysts in the social sciences are to become more than ideological "hit men" employed by interest groups wishing to protect their turf, these problems must be overcome. In the absence of truly objective criteria and rational assessment of public policy, the public sector will be continuously buffeted by the prevailing ideological winds. If we are to achieve greater professionalism and objectivity in the public sector, biases such as those attributed to political ideology must be identified and controlled. Only then will we avoid the tragedy of implementing poorly conceived policy, an outcome that occurs all too often in the public sector.

NOTES

1. Woodrow Wilson, "The Study of Administration," in *Classics of Public Administration*, ed. Jay Shafritz and Albert Hyde (Oak Park, Ill.: Moore Publishing Company, 1978), pp. 3–17.

2. John Rex, ed., *From Max Weber: Essays in Sociology* (London: Routledge and Kegan Paul, 1982), p. 145.

3. Theodore Poister, *Public Program Analysis* (Baltimore: University Park Press, 1978), p. 21.

4. Diane Ravitch, *The Revisionists Revised* (New York: Basic Books, 1977), pp. 99, 173.

5. Michael Engel, *State and Local Politics Fundamentals & Perspectives* (New York: St. Martin's Press, 1985), pp. 382–85.

6. Anthony Lewis, "Rigid Ideology Fouls the Debate on AIDS, Central America, Bork," *Des Moines Register*, 13 October 1987, p. 6A.

7. Patricia W. Ingraham, "Building Bridges or Burning Them? The President, the Appointees, and the Bureaucracy," *Public Administration Review* 47, no. 5 (September–October 1987): 425–35.

8. James P. Pfiffner, "Political Appointees and Career Executives: The Democracy-Bureaucracy Nexus in the Third Century," *Public Administration Review* 47, no. 1 (January–February 1987): 57–65.

9. Ibid., p. 63.

10. "Volcker Will Head New Panel on Civil Service," *Public Administration Times* 10, no. 16 (21 August 1987), p. 5.

Bibliography

Achor, Shirly. *Mexican Americans in a Dallas Barrio* (Tucson: University of Arizona Press, 1978).

Babbie, Earl. *The Practice of Social Research* (Belmont, Calif.: Wadsworth, 1983).

Bahl, Roy, Campbell, Alan, and Greytak, David. *Taxes, Expenditures and the Economic Base: A Case Study of New York City* (New York: Praeger, 1974).

Baradat, Leon. *Political Ideologies* (Englewood Cliffs, N.J.: Prentice-Hall, 1979).

Barone, Michael and Ujifusa, Grant, eds. *The Almanac of American Politics* (Washington, D.C.: National Journal, 1983).

Bell, Daniel. *The End of Ideology* (New York: Free Press, 1960).

Blumberg, Barbara. *The New Deal and the Unemployed* (Cranbury, N.J.: Associated University Press, 1979).

Bramsted, E. K. and Melhuish, K. J., eds. *Western Liberalism* (London: The Chaucer Press, 1978).

Braybrook, David and Lindblom, Charles. *A Strategy of Decision* (New York: Free Press, 1970).

Briggs, Asa. "The Welfare State in Historical Perspective," in M. Zald, ed., *Social Welfare Institutions* (New York: John Wiley & Sons, 1965).

Buchanan, James. "The Pure Theory of Government Finance: A Suggested Approach," *Journal of Political Economy* 57 (December 1949).

Campbell, Angus, Converse, Phillip, Miller, Warren, and Stokes, Donald. *The American Voter* (New York: John Wiley & Sons, 1964).

Caraley, Demetrious. *City Governments and Urban Problems* (Englewood Cliffs, N.J.: Prentice-Hall, 1977).

Carnegie, Andrew. "Wealth," *North American Review* (June 1889).

Christenson, Reo, Engel, Alan, Jacobs, Dan, Rejai, Mostafa, and Herbert, Walter. *Ideologies and Modern Politics* (London: Thomas Nelson & Sons, 1971).

De Tocqueville, Alexis. *Democracy in America* (New York: New American Library, 1956).

Diggins, John. *American Political Thought* (New York: Holt, Rinehart and Winston, 1960).

Dolbeare, Kenneth and Dolbeare, Patricia. *American Ideologies The Competing Beliefs of the 1970's* (Chicago: Rand McNally, 1978).

Downs, Anthony. *An Economic Theory of Democracy* (New York: Harper & Row, 1957).

Drucker, A. M. *The Political Uses of Ideology* (New York: Harper & Row, 1974).

Ebenstein, William. *Today's ISMS* (Englewood Cliffs, N.J.: Prentice-Hall, 1964).

Eccleshall, Robert, Geoghegan, Vincent, Richard, Jay, and Wilford, Rick. *Political Ideologues* (London: Hutchinson & Co., 1984).

Elazar, Daniel. *American Federalism: A View from the States* (New York: Thomas Crowell, 1972).

Engel, Michael. *State and Local Politics Fundamentals & Perspectives* (New York: St. Martin's Press, 1985).

Etzioni-Halevy, Eva. *Bureaucracy and Democracy—A Political Dilemma* (London: Routledge and Kegan Paul, 1983).

Feuer, Lewis. *Ideology and the Ideologists* (Oxford: Basil Blackwell, 1975).

First National City Bank. *Profile of a City* (New York: McGraw-Hill, 1972).

Francis, Samuel. "Message from MARS: The Social Politics of the New Right," in R. Whitaker, ed., *The New Right Papers* (New York: St. Martin's Press, 1982).

Friedman, Milton and Friedman, Rose. *Free to Choose* (New York: Avon Books, 1979).

Freeden, Michael. *The New Liberalism: An Ideology of Social Reform* (Oxford: Oxford University Press, 1978).

Fusfeld, Daniel. *The Age of the Economist* (Glenview, Ill.: Scott, Foresman, 1982).

Gerth, H. H. and Mills, C. Wright. *From Max Weber: Essays in Sociology* (London: Routledge and Kegan Paul, 1948).

Gilder, George. *Wealth and Poverty* (New York: Basic Books, 1981).

Greytak, David, Phares, Donald, and Morley, Elaine. *Municipal Output and Performance in New York City* (Lexington, Mass.: D. C. Heath, 1976).

Grimes, Alan. *American Political Thought* (New York: Holt, Rinehart and Winston, 1960).

Halperin, Morton. *Bureaucratic Politics and Foreign Policy* (Washington, D.C.: The Brookings Institution, 1965).

Harrigan, John. *Political Change in the Metropolis* (Boston: Little, Brown, 1985).

Harrington, Michael, "Why the Welfare State Breaks Down," in I. Howe, ed., *Beyond the Welfare State* (New York: Schocken Books, 1982).

Hartman, Robert, "Congress and Budget-Making," in B. Bozeman and J. Straussman, eds., *New Directions in Public Administration* (Belmont, Calif.: Brooks/Cole, 1984).

Hartz, Louis. *The Liberal Tradition in America* (New York: Harcourt, Brace & World, 1955).

Haveman, Robert. *The Economics of the Public Sector* (New York: John Wiley & Sons, 1976).

Heidenheimer, Arnold, Heclo, Hugh, and Adams, Carolyn. *Comparative Public Policy: The Politics of Social Choice in Europe and America* (New York: St. Martin's Press, 1983).

Hook, Sidney, "A New ISM for Socialism," pp. 325–30 in W. J. Stankiewicz, ed., *Political Thought since World War II* (New York: Free Press, 1964).

Hoover, Kenneth. *Ideology and Political Life* (Monterey, Calif.: Brooks/Cole, 1986).

Hoy, Robert, "Lid on a Boiling Pot," in R. Whitaker, ed., *The New Right Papers* (New York: St. Martin's Press, 1982).

Ingersoll, David. *Communism, Fascism and Democracy* (Columbus, Oh.: Charles E. Merrill, 1971).

Ingraham, Patricia. "Building Bridges or Burning Them? The President, the Appointees, and the Bureaucracy," *Public Administration Review* 47, no. 5 (September–October 1987).

Jorstad, Erling. *The Politics of Moralism* (Minneapolis: Augsbert Publishing House, 1981).

Jun, Jong S. "Management by Objectives in the Public Sector," *Public Administration Review* 36 (January–February 1976).

Key, V. O., Jr. "The Lack of a Budgetary Theory," *American Political Science Review* 34 (December 1940).

Koven, Steven. "The Impact of Political Ideology on Socioeconomic and Budgetary Dynamics." Unpublished dissertation. University of Florida, 1982.

Kristol, Irving. *Two Cheers for Capitalism* (New York: Basic Books, 1978).

Ladd, Everett C. *The American Polity The People and Their Government* (New York: W. W. Norton, 1987).

Lee, Robert and Johnson, Ronald. *Public Budgeting Systems* (Baltimore: University Park Press, 1983).

Leslie, Warren. *Dallas Public and Private* (New York: Grossman Publishers, 1964).

Lewis, Verne. "Toward a Theory of Budgeting," *Public Administration Review* 12 (Winter 1952): 42–54.

Levy, Michael. *Political Thought in America* (Homewood, Ill.: The Dorsey Press, 1982).

Lowi, Theodore. *The End of Liberalism* (New York: W. W. Norton, 1969).

MacLeod, Celeste. *Horatio Alger, Farewell: The End of the American Dream* (New York: Seaview Books, 1980).

Macpherson, C. B. "The False Roots of Western Democracy," in Fred R. Dallmayr, ed., *From Contract to Community* (New York: Marcel Dekker, 1978).

Mandel, Ernest. *An Introduction to Marxist Economic Theory* (New York: Pathfinder Press, 1969).

Mannheim, Karl. *Ideology and Utopia* (London: Routledge and Kegan Paul, 1936).

Merget, Astrid. "The Era of Fiscal Restraint," in *The 1980 Municipal Yearbook* (Washington, D.C.: The International City Management Association, 1980).

Metcalf, Linda and Dolbeare, Kenneth. *Neopolitics American Political Ideas in the 1980s* (Philadelphia: Temple University Press, 1985).

Meyer, Alfred G. *Communism* (New York: Random House, 1984).

Mills, Gregory, "The Budget: A Failure of Discipline," in John Palmer and Isabel Sawhill, eds., *The Reagan Record* (Cambridge, Mass.: Ballinger, 1984).

Mises, Ludwig von. *Bureaucracy* (New Haven: Yale University Press, 1944).

Musgrave, Richard. "The Voluntary Exchange Theory of Public Economy," *Quarterly Journal of Economics* (February 1939): 213-17.

Musgrave, Richard and Musgrave, Peggy. *Public Finance in Theory and Practice*, 4th ed. (New York: McGraw-Hill, 1984).

Ott, David and Ott, Attiat. *Federal Budget Policy* (Washington, D.C.: The Brookings Institution, 1965).

Palmer, John and Sawhill, Isabel, eds. *The Reagan Record* (Cambridge, Mass.: Ballinger, 1984).

Peters, Charles. "A Neoliberal's Manifesto," *The Washington Monthly*, May 1983.

Pfiffner, James. "Political Appointees and Career Executives: The Democracy-Bureaucracy Nexus in the Third Century," *Public Administration Review* 47, no. 1 (January–February 1987): 57-65.

Poister, Theodore. *Public Program Analysis* (Baltimore: University Park Press, 1978).

Podhoretz, Norman. *Breaking Ranks* (New York: Harper & Row, 1979).

Pyhrr, Peter. "The Zero-Base Approach to Government Budgeting," *Public Administration Review* 37 (January–February 1977): 1-18.

Ranney, Austin. *Governing An Introduction to Political Science* (Englewood Cliffs, N.J.: Prentice-Hall, 1987).

Ravitch, Diane. *The Revisionists Revised* (New York: Basic Books, 1977).

Rejai, Mostafa. *Comparative Political Ideologies* (New York: St. Martin's Press, 1984).

Revel, Jean-François. *The Totalitarian Temptation* (New York: Doubleday, 1977).

Rex, John, ed. *From Max Weber, Essays in Sociology* (London: Routledge and Kegan Paul, 1982).

Riis, Jacob. *The Children of the Poor* (New York: Garrett Press, 1979).
———. *How the Other Half Lives* (New York: Charles Scribner's Sons, 1980).
Rose, Richard. "Implementation and Evaluation: The Record of MBO," in F. Kramer, ed., *Contemporary Approaches to Public Budgeting* (Cambridge: Winthrop, 1979).
Rothenberg, Randall. "The Neoliberal Club," *Esquire*, February 1982.
Rourke, Francis E. *Bureaucracy, Politics and Public Policy* (Boston: Little, Brown, 1984).
Saeger, Richard. *American Government and Politics A Neoconservative Approach* (Glenview, Ill.: Scott, Foresman, 1982).
Samuelson, Paul. "The Pure Theory of Public Expenditures," *Review of Economics and Statistics* 36 (November 1954): 387-89.
Sargent, Lyman T. *Contemporary Political Ideologies* (Homewood, Ill.: The Dorsey Press, 1981).
Schick, Allan. "The Road to PPB: The Stages of Budget Reform," *Public Administration Review* 26 (December 1966): 243-58.
———. "Zero-Base Budgeting and Sunset: Redundancy or Symbiosis?" *The Bureaucrat* 6 (Spring 1977): 12-32.
———. "The Road from ZBB," *Public Administration Review* 38 (March-April 1978): 177-80.
Sharkansky, Ira. *The Politics of Taxing and Spending* (New York: Bobbs-Merrill, 1969).
Steinfels, Peter. *The Neoconservatives The Men Who Are Changing America's Politics* (New York: Simon and Schuster, 1980).
Stockman, David. *The Triumph of Politics* (New York: Harper & Row, 1986).
Straussman, Jeffrey. *Public Administration* (New York: CBS College Publishing, 1985).
Sweezy, Paul. "Vietnam: Endless War," in M. Gottleman and D. Mermelstein, eds., *The Failure of American Liberalism* (New York: Vintage Books, 1970), p. 594.
Thompson, Dennis. *The Democratic Citizen* (London: Cambridge University Press, 1970).
Tiebout, Charles. "A Pure Theory of Local Expenditures," *Journal of Political Economy* 64 (October 1956): 416-24.
Tosi, Henry and Carroll, Stephen. "Management by Objective," in Jay Shafritz, ed., *A New World: Readings on Modern Public Personnel Management* (Chicago: International Personnel Management Association, 1975).

Truman, David. *The Governmental Process* (New York: Alfred A. Knopf, 1951).

Viguerie, Richard. "Ends and Means," in R. Whitaker, ed., *The New Right Papers* (New York: St. Martin's Press, 1982).

Wanniski, Jude. *The Way the World Works* (New York: Basic Books, 1981).

Watkins, Frederick. *The Age of Ideology-Political Thought, 1950 to Present* (Englewood Cliffs, N.J.: Prentice-Hall, 1964).

Weiss, Carol. "The Many Meanings of Research Utilization," in E. Chelimsky, ed., *Program Evaluation: Patterns and Directions* (Washington, D.C.: The American Society for Public Administration, 1985).

Weyrich, Paul. "Blue Collar or Blue Blood: The New Right Compared to the Old Right," in R. Whitaker, ed., *The New Right Papers* (New York: St. Martin's Press, 1982).

Wildavsky, Aaron. "Rescuing Policy Analysis from PPBS," *Public Administration Review* 29 (March-April 1969).

———. *The Politics of the Budgetary Process* (Boston: Little, Brown, 1984).

———. "The Political Implications of Budgetary Reform," *Public Administration Review* 21 (Autumn 1961): 183-90.

Wilson, Peter. *The Future of Dallas Capital Plant* (Washington, D.C.: The Urban Institute, 1980).

Wilson, Woodrow. "The Study of Administration," in J. Shafritz and A. Hyde, eds., *Classics of Public Administration* (Oak Park, Ill.: Moore Publishing Company, 1978).

Wright, Diel. *Understanding Intergovernmental Relations* (North Scituate, Mass.: Duxbury Press, 1978).

Index

ABOUT THE AUTHOR

STEVEN G. KOVEN was born in New York City and attended the City College of New York, receiving a bachelor's degree in business administration in 1968. Following graduation, he served in the United States military which included a tour of duty in Vietnam. Upon returning to the United States, he was employed in various federal agencies including the Department of Health, Education, and Welfare and the Department of Commerce. Koven received a master's degree in business administration from Baruch College (CUNY) in 1975 and a Ph.D. in political science from the University of Florida in 1982. Since 1982 he has been teaching American government and public administration. He spent two years (1985–1986) in Europe as a professor of public administration at Troy State University-Europe. Currently, Dr. Koven is teaching American government and public administration at Iowa State University.